COMPREHENSIVE
MEMORY
DEVELOPMENT
COURSE

Authored by

Dr. B. K. Chandra Shekhar

(Guinness World Record Holder)

MA (Eco), M Sc (Yoga), M Sc (Psycho Neurobics), PGDY,
PG Diploma (Memory Development & Psycho Neurobics),
Ph. D (Alternative Medicine)

V&S PUBLISHERS

Published by:

V&S PUBLISHERS

F-2/16, Ansari Road, Daryaganj, New Delhi-110002
011-23240026, 011-23240027 • *Fax:* 011-23240028
Email: info@vspublishers.com • *Website:* www.vspublishers.com

Branch : Hyderabad
5-1-707/1, Brij Bhawan (Beside Central Bank of India Lane)
Bank Street, Koti, Hyderabad - 500 095
040-24737290
E-mail: vspublishershyd@gmail.com

Branch Offi ce Mumbai
Godown # 34 at The Model Co-Operative Housing, Society Ltd.,
"Sahakar Niwas", Ground Floor, Next to Sobo Central, Mumbai - 400 034
022-23510736
E-mail vspublishersmum@gmail.com

Follow us on: [t] [f] [in]

All books available at **www.vspublishers.com**

Printed at : Unique Colour Carton, New Delhi-110020

Dedication

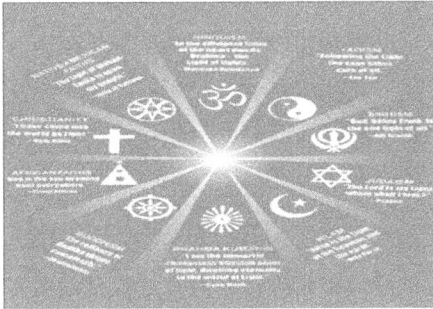

This book is dedicated to the most revered Supreme God Father Shiva, who disclosed the knowledge of mind and memory power of Head Top Computer to me. I also dedicate this book to my daughter – Khushi (alias "Pari"), who is the source of constant inspiration and creative writing.

Publisher's Note

- *Do you find it difficult to recall names, faces, phone numbers or text matter from any academic or other field you have been acquainted with?*

- *How often do you experience the embarrassment of forgetting the next few lines during an important lecture?*

- *Don't you shake your head mentally ashamed at your inability to recall the text you have studied?*

If your answer is *yes* to any of the above questions, then your memory needs some work. We may conclude, 'You have a bad memory.' It's time to take shelter under the watchful guidance of **Dr. B. K. Chandra Shekhar**, Guinness World Record Holder and an ideologue on mind sharpening, with his life-changing book named – **Comprehensive Memory Development Course**.

Using various time-tested scientific as well as innovative techniques, the author in this inimitable book explains how to remember names, facts, events, and almost any academic and non-academic information with simple yet powerful methods that are simple enough even for a child.

This comprehensive book on memory development will allow us to achieve what we always desire – a sharp memory. The book is divided into sections which give ideas on different memory enhancement methods, such as, rhyme method, shape method, value method, phonetic method, mnemonics, link method, mental pegs, etc. The techniques to remember names, place, location, phone, etc., are explained. The best part for students is the applications of memory methods to remember subjects like, geography, history, social studies, articles, physics, chemistry, biology, management studies, civil services subjects, etc. A whole section has been devoted to explaining psycho neurobic exercises for developing mind and memory power.

On the whole, the treatment delivered here has been such that the reader learns the effective techniques on how to maintain the brain in top condition, how to overcome forgetfulness, and how to easily retain data and figures and information in the mind for immediate retrieval at any desired time.

Get ready to upgrade the mental faculty to memorise numbers, facts, course materials and other information like never before.

Acknowledgements

At the outset, I thank my Almighty father-GOD, the father of humanity pita Shri Brahma Baba and my Divine mother Jagdamba Saraswati, who have taught me the concept of head top computer and programmed the treasures of knowledge and wisdom in my memory. I express my deep gratitude to Air Marshal P. S. Bhangu, PVSM, AVSM, VM (Retd) for motivating me and writing the foreword for this book. I am also thankful to my Memory Guru Dr. Biswaroop Roy Chowdhury and his spouse Mrs. Neerja Roy Chowdhury for all encouragement and supports.

I specially thank my younger brother Vijay Shankar Tiwari and Vidyawati for helping in writing and editing of this book. I specially thank my elder angelic brother Rajkumarjee, angelic guide Chanda and angelic sister Sonu (Son Pari) for constant supports and motivation. I also thank Shikhar Taneja, Kanika Taneja, Renu Mishra, Munish Kaushal, Dibya Bora (the former editor) and the young, energetic CEO of V&S Publishers, Mr. Sahil Gupta, who has brought out the book so soon and so decently.

I am also thankful to my parents (Father – Shri Braj Kishore Tiwari and Mother – Smt. Sumanti Devi) and family members (wife – Reeta and duaghter – Khushi), my younger brother Shiv Shanker Tiwari for all the help and their best wishes.

– Dr. B. K. Chandra Shekhar
Email: bkcshekhar@gmail.com
Website: www.invisibledoctor.com
www.sigfasolutions.com

Foreword

Memory development skill is directly related to creative intellect. Intellect is a faculty of soul through which it selects the desired thoughts and emotions. The intellect performs three important functions, i.e. to visualise, to discriminate and to decide. Out of these, the power to visualise is the most important function of the intellect. Memory development is the result of creative visualisation power of intellect.

Air Marshal P. S. Bhangu, PVSM, AVSM, VM (Retd)

A soul with a powerful intellect can enjoy the experience of its own choice regardless of external stimuli, whereas a soul with a weak intellect is often pushed by the strong impressions or habits stored in subconscious mind. It can also be influenced by the moods of the other or by atmosphere around. That is why many psychologists say that our subconscious mind/ unconscious mind is very powerful and it gets things done automatically. Memory development means programming subconscious or unconscious mind.

This book is comprehensive in nature that provides very interesting techniques on developing the memory skills. This book surpasses other write-ups on this subjects in following aspects:

1. This book, comprehensively analyses the human memory system with respect to the power of soul, whereas other books relate the function of memory entirely with the process of the brain mechanism only. Brain is just an instrument for recording but the mind and intellect play the vital role in memory programming.

2. This book systematically presents the techniques of memory programming with special focus on students' requirements. This book is very helpful for students and can be easily grasped by them. The technique taught in this book would be a great help to anyone besides students.

Dr. B. K. Chandra Shekhar is known to me personally for the last seven years. He is a simple man with high thinking. He has lots of experience of applying the power of third eye. He applied these powers to get rid of life threatening diseases like cancer, hepatitis and diabetes. His services are sought from various schools, colleges, social organisations, institutions and Central/State govts. He conducts memory workshops for students and professionals. He also provides very useful guidance to students to remove their exam fear and better their performances.

He has put sincere efforts to present this precious knowledge of memory system in a book form worth emulating for the benefits of student community. His efforts are an eye opener for all of us. I hope this book will certainly prove beneficial for the student in opening their third eye and in enhancing their memory power and help them to harness their talents and release their true potential. I wish him in this hard endeavour and many successes in his life.

– Air Marshal P. S. Bhangu
Email: minpaj@hotmail.com

Contents

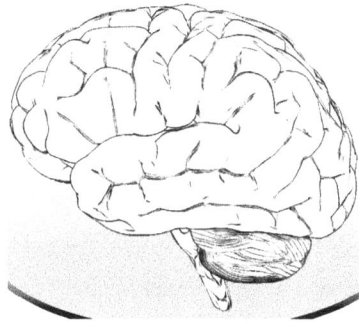

Introduction

The concept of human mind and memory is a complex phenomenon, beyond the scope of modern science. Since science is basically concerned with the physical universe, it deals with the matter and not with the spiritual aspects. Hence, modern science is not capable of explaining the truths of life beyond matter. There is a tendency to reject whatever cannot be understood through materialistic reasoning and logic. Ocasioanally, what cannot be explained in normal life is also attributed to God, the supreme power.

There are two channels in the acquisition of knowledge. One is knowledge gathered through

is alive and continued to remain physical world – oriented, one can experience only transient happiness. Our association with the world is because of the physical body. The human mind remains busy in with sensuous pleasures and completely ignores the purpose of our incarnation. It is high time for our dormant mind to awake now.

the awakening and enlightening of the mind take place, lies beneath the normal mental awareness. Logic and normal reasoning do not bind it. By activating the standard software of the intuitive mind or conscience (also called sub- conscious mind) the truths of life can

the intuitive mind or conscience or you can say "the third eye". Albert Einstein had admitted that his theory of relativity was gained with the help of intuitive mind or "the third eye".

beyond. This is the base of our memory. The vast reservoir of rational knowledge possessed by the most learned persons today fails to explain the truths of life and solutions to life's problems.

NEED OF MEMORY

A number of people remain skeptical about the potential of the human brain, pointing to the substandard performances that many of us routinely churn out. Consider the following aspect of education, which is not given to students in the schools, colleges or universities.

Brain, its function and memory power

Memory techniques

Function of mind

Difference between mind and brain

Application of study technique in day-to-day student life

How to develop concentration power

How to motivate self.

How to take examinations.

The power of Third Eye for vivid visualisation.

How to develop creativity and so on.

The reason our performances do not match our potential is simply because we are given no information about what we are or about how we can best utilise our inherent qualities. Hence, understanding these basic concepts and techniques of memory will help us to match our performance with our inherent potential and explore our memory.

From the moment we're born, we're learning. Learning, however, would be useless if we didn't have a way to store all the information we're learning and then access it later. Fortunately, memory takes care of that – memory allows us to process information, store information, and then access it later when we need it.

This may sound very simple, but it's actually quite complex. But have no fear; we'll break it down for you, so it's not too tough.

You can think of human memory like a library. The purpose of a library is to store books,

materials so they can be retrieved later. If books wear out from excessive use or get lost, they need to be replaced. Libraries obtain new books and materials every year that also need to be

make room for new ones.

SHORT-TERM MEMORY

Short term memory allows a person to recall something after a short period of time without practicing or rehearsing. George Miller wrote a paper on short term memory called "The magical number 7 ± 2." He concluded from his experiments that we could retain 5 to 9 items with our short term memory without rehearsal. The amount can be increased if items are "chunked" together. Most people remember phone numbers in three chunked sets – the area code, the

degrades and becomes lost unless it is repeated or rehearsed.

LONG-TERM MEMORY

Long term memory refers to retention of information over the long term from days to years. There are 2 types of long term memory; objective memory and subjective memory. Conscious mind and intellect both are known as objective memory – because it deals with outward objects. The objective memory is aware of the objective world. Its media of observation is our physical sense. Our intellect, one of the faculties of objective mind, is our guide and director in

memory works through observation, education and its association with past experiences of memory.The greatest function of the objective memory is performed by intellect that is of reasoning, visualising and decision making.

Subconscious memory is also referred as subjective memory. It is aware of its environment, but not by means of physical senses. It perceives by intuition. It is the seat of emotions and the storehouse of memory. It performs the highest functions when our objective senses are not functioning. In other words, it is that intelligence that makes itself known when the objective memory is suspended or in a sleepy or drowsy state or in alpha, or delta state.

For example, riding a bike would be considered an objective memory. Remembering something that happened as a child would be subjective memory.

There is no limit to how much information a person can store in long term memory although various brain disorders and damage can prevent or slow the process. Many techniques can aid and increase the likelihood that information will be retained long term. The next section will illustrate different ways to memorise and strengthen retention of information as well as describe some reasons why we may forget things.

result in our studies... but they must be very strong and organised. If it is not so; they will take us nowhere. Mostly students memorise any subject in a rote method "in Hindi, we call it

" (parrot memory). In rote method of memorisation, thoughts or information are most of the time unorganised and students blindly mug up the answers... they repeat the things until the material is registered in their subconscious mind. Whenever they are asked a question,

Remember, how many times we commit ourselves to memorising all the tables or equations or maps or the long questions answers, and then we mug them up blindly, hours later, when we try

more and more revisions and still there is no guarantee of perfect and timely recall.

Though hard work is must and there is no substitute for it, however, in today's competition era, you cannot win with hard work alone. There are techniques to help us in competitions, and to memorising all subjects, i.e. science, maths, physics, etc., these techniques are based on visualisation and they can make learning easy. According to these techniques, you can keep any information perfectly in your mind if you can convert it into mental pictures.

When we forget things, it is often a problem of encoding. Perhaps we were distracted while trying to learn information or while we were doing something. For instance, how many times you have lost your keys or misplaced the remote control? Perhaps you were thinking

while memory requires conscious attention. Thus, distraction explains why you put your keys in the refrigerator and threw the remote control in the garbage can.

Perhaps you weren't distracted but also didn't make enough associations to strengthen the memory of where you put your keys. This leads to an inability to retrieve the memory of where you left them. You may be able to imagine several possible places they could be but can't quite remember which. A common solution to this is to "retrace your steps." In essence, "retracing

that is connected to the keys' location.

All information can't be sent to long term memory, because our memory is like a pet child. It will not accept information unless it is provided by the special language in which it understands, i.e. by certain technique. Generally memory or you can say it subconscious mind does' not receive if the information is provided at the rate in which conscious mind receives. There may arise some problems while memorising due to:

    Incapability of the conscious mind

    Incapable of memorising anything by the right method.

    Due to absent-mindedness

Yes, people with excellent memory can also be absent-minded. Here is a popular anecdote about absent-mindedness.

Louis Pasteur was dining at home with his friends. When his table companions were about to eat the grapes served for dessert, Pasteur stopped them by saying, 'there is nothing as dangerous

then explained to them all the bacilli and microbes that may be found in a cluster of grapes.

Everybody listen raptly, but suddenly, the spell was broken by a general burst of laughter. The scientist had unconsciously picked up the glass of water in which he had drowned so many germs and taken one long swallow. Pasteur was not the last to laugh at his absent-mindedness.

So, absent-mindedness is nothing more than in attention. If pay attention to anything, we will remember it.

Remember our eyes cannot see when our mind is absent.

Many times we experience that when we start listening to a lecture in the classroom with full

learn the techniques to memorise and retain the things for a longer period in the forthcoming chapters.

When Albert Einstein died, his brain was brought in a laboratory and was examined meticulously comparing it with a common man's brain. On comparison it was found that there existed no dissimilarities of even .001%. Both the brains were exactly similar. Then what made Albert Einstein's brain so special? It was the Einstein's being, which utilised more than 10% of his brain's trillions of neurons. Invisible doctor uses physical brain, which is the hardware of his head top computer.

Head top computer of the soul consists of brain, which is the hardware and universal laws, which are the standard software. Soul through its faculites (Mind, Intellect and Sanskar) automatically operates this computer (we call it head top computer because it is in the head of all human beings) within the universal laws to

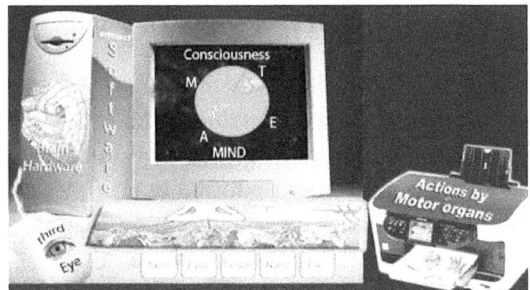

human brain is a paired organ; it is composed of two halves, called cerebral hemispheres. The theory of the structure and functions of the brain suggests that the two sides of the brain control two different modes of thinking. Just stop to wonder for a moment, how a two-year-old baby can master the task of speaking so effortlessly, while most adult's efforts of learning a foreign language tend to end up as more of confusion and less learning. Most children are born with dominant right hemisphere. When an infant learns a language, he/she does so with all senses, such as those of smell, sound, colours and touch. As we grow older, the left hemisphere's mode of thinking, which relies heavily on partial processes (without visualisation) of the intellect, such as logic, sequence and organisation, become dominant. In the Zen tradition, the left mind is associated with the process of thinking and the right mind is associated with knowing. Most individuals tend to have a distinct preference for one or the other side of the brain. From very early in life, school and society too conspire to identify individual as having preference for either Arts or Science and thus label them as being "Creative or logical".

Soul through its one of the faculties, i.e Mind uses left hemisphere of brain for logical and verbal reasoning. It deals with words, analysis (breaking a part of word or sentence) and sequential thinking. Mind uses right hemisphere of brain for intuition, creativity, dealing with pictures, synthesis (putting together) and holistic thinking. Brain itself does not do anything. In the absence of mind (conscious life force) brain is called dead. Right hemisphere of brain is mostly used by the intellect's creative power and visualisation power (third eye). Do not confuse mind with brain. Both are two different things. Mind is the faculty of soul whereas the brain is the part of our physical body.

	Mind		Brain
1.	It is Metaphysical (faculty of Soul)	1.	It is physical (Part of body)
2.	It is the software of the human computer.	2.	It is the hardware of human computer.
3.	There are three faculties of the Soul – Mind, Intellect & Impressions.	3.	There are two parts of the brain (Left and Right). Left is used for analysis, Right is used for creativity.
4.	It is weightless.	4.	It's weight is approx 2% of body weight.

TYPES OF BRAIN WAVES

Thought is an energy, which is created in conscious mind by the input of either sense organs or memories. When thoughts enter into the brain, brain waves are created. Thoughts can be compared to stones or pebbles and brain can be compared to a pond. When pebbles or stones (thoughts) are thrown into the pond (brain) ripples called brain waves are created. Thoughts are also similar to electrical current. When an electrical current enters into a wire, a wave of frequency 50 Hz is created in the wire. These waves are categorised as per their frequency and voltage. These are:

a. **Alpha Waves:** These are moderately fast (8 to 13 cycles per sec) and are relatively high voltage waves. Normally, EEG records these waves when an individual is awake, has his eyes closed and is in a relaxed state and his cerebrum is idling so to say. It keeps our mind and body in relaxed and receptive state. It is having a vast potential for performance. Alpha state of mind triggers our standard impressions of memory.

b. **Beta Waves:** These are comparatively faster (13 to 25 cycles per sec) than alpha waves but in amplitude they are lower in voltage. Beta waves are obtained when an individual is awake, has his eyes open, and is in an activated or attentive state, that is to say, when his cerebrum is not idling but is busily engaged with sensory stimulation and mental stimulation. Brain is just like a pond, where water is still and one can see one's faces very clearly as there are no ripples on the surface of water. Thoughts and emotions can be compared to pebbles and stones. When these pebbles and stones are thrown into the pond there are several ripples created on the surface of water due to agitations caused by the stones. Similarly, when pebbles and stones of thoughts and emotions from our metaphysical mind enter into the pond of physical brain, agitations in the brain are caused and different types of brain waves are created depending upon the nature of (size) pebbles and stones of thoughts and emotions from mind entering into the brain. One cycle in one second is called one Htz.

Beta Waves are further categorised as follows:

1. **Normal Range:** Between 13 and 18 Hz. This is triggered by routine impressions. In this state we are busy and active. Biochemistry, hormones and enzymes levels remain within normal range. Continuing in beta waves gives sign of tiredness.

2. **Abnormal Range:** Between 18 and 25 Hz. Thoughts of waste impressions of our memory bank trigger these waves. Biochemistry and secretion of hormones and enzymes get affected. Tiredness and stress increases. Disturbance in easiness of mind causes diseases in body.

3. **Most Abnormal Range:** Between 25 and 50 Hz. Thoughts of negative impressions of our memory bank trigger these waves and further cause distress and depressions in life. All types of diseases start, immune system gets weakened. Brain cells and capillaries get ruptured which further cause brain hemorrhage and paralysis.

4. **Deranged Range (beyond50 Hz):** Sign of mental disorder and madness. It also indicates loss of memory.

c. **Theta Waves:** These are moderately slow (3 to 7Hz) and low voltage waves that predominate when drowsiness descends. This is a dream state. Consciousness never functions but intellect keeps functioning with uncontrolled visualisations of images from subconscious mind. All randomly recorded images (Recorded by electronic or print media and by visualisation of waste and negative images during awake state) get opened during dream state, which makes our brain to work during sleep. This lowers the potential and creates a low voltage. This further gives tiredness despite sleeping more.

d. **Delta Waves:** These are the lowest (0.5 to 3Hz) brain waves and they have a high voltage. They are recorded when an individual is in deep sleep. Because of this fact, the physiologists refer to deep sleep as Slow Wave Sleep (SWS). This is the deep state of sleep that gives complete relaxation to our mind, intellect and body. Our mind and body get charged due to deep relaxation. Constant state of delta waves triggers our standard impressions, which renew us physically, mentally and spiritually. All inventions take place during this concentrated state of mind. Mystery of the universe sometimes gets revealed during dream waves between 3.5 to 4 Hz. If the EEG indicates that the

that the individual is dead.

Function of Head Top Computer (HTC) and its relationship with the operator:

A. Software for HTC is impressed in the Standard Files of Memory Bank (Subconscious mind). This software is related to the following:

Regulation of heartbeat, blood circulation, pulse rate, respiration, maintaining body temperature, standard secretion of hormones and enzymes, maintaining normal biochemistry of blood, digestion, assimilation (transmitting food into tissue, blood muscles, bones etc.) and controlling of all vital functions. It starts working automatically through the involuntary actions of the autonomic nervous system, from the day the soul enters into a human body. No one teaches it. It is an in-built mechanism within the memory of the soul, which functions without a remote control and round the clock whether we are awake or asleep. The basic qualities (primary virtues) of the soul are that of knowledge, peace, purity, love, joy, bliss and power, along with Secondary virtues such as harmony, honesty, maturity, politeness, etc. It is a vast source of our ideals, aspirations and altruistic urges. It has a solution to all our problems and vast information about creativity, art,

sense or intuitive mind/ spiritual powers / higher consciousness / supra consciousness.

Bank (Impressions of Routine Work) in coordination with standard software. Information related to daily routine works on day-to-day activities.

PART : 1

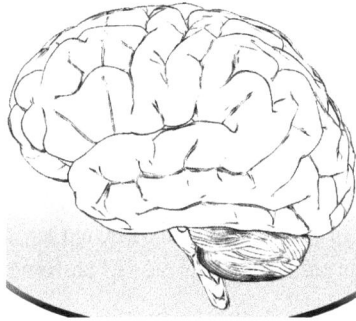

LAWS of MEMORY

Chapter 1

DATA STORAGE OR MEMORY BANK

Now let us see the last system of being – "The Memory System". (Its faculties are Subconscious mind and Unconscious mind, which can be called memory bank). Impressions of every action, observation and imagination in Subconscious Mind and unconscious mind are called Memory. The memory bank or the treasures of impressions are known as "Sanskar". The Psychoanalysts say that it is the sleeping mind or involuntary mind or even female mind.

WHAT IS A MEMORY BANK?

(It is also known as treasures of subconscious and unconscious mind)

1. **It is our inner garden:** This storehouse is also known as a garden. Soul is the gardener. As the soul plants the seeds of thoughts with the help of an implement known as intellect, in the garden of Subconscious mind, so shall it reap in the future. Imagine your subconscious

   a rose garden. Every thought is cause and every condition is an effect. This is the reason it is so essential that you take charge of your thoughts through enhanced power of third eye. Now begin to sow thoughts of peace, happiness, right action, good will and prosperity. Think quietly and with conviction on these qualities. Continue to plant these wonderful seeds of thought in the garden of your subconscious mind and you will reap a glorious harvest. Once you begin to control your thought processes with the help of your intellect, you can apply

   repeatedly say to your memory bank, "I cannot do it," your memory will create the same environment in the body and mind and you will feel incapable of doing it.

2. **It is like Software of Human Computer:** Let us understand this with one more example. Your body is like a ship. You are the navigator of the ship. You navigate this ship with the computerised cabin devices. This cabin can be compared to the brain of the body. The software in these computerised devices is known as memory data. As you press the required button, so is the response from these devices, which create conditions for smooth navigation. Similarly, your memory bank receives order from you through conscious

mind and intellect and it responds accordingly through physical body for navigating life in the ocean of the world. Be sure, your subconscious mind follows only your orders. If you press the button of fear, worry and anxiety through the thought system of your conscious mind and visualise the same things through your third eye (the Intellect), your subconscious mind or memory banks will act accordingly and will activate fear

the mind).

3. **It is the Basis of our Consciousness:** Subconscious mind or Impressions (   ) is a major manifestation of human consciousness (soul). It can be compared to a receptacle that contains habits, tendencies, personality traits, memories, values, beliefs, learning, talents, instincts, etc. The qualities of activities of the other two manifestations of human soul, i.e. mind and intellect environment are based on the quality of   is the

4. **It is the Archives of All Previously Recorded Experiences:** It is the store of the complete data of the soul's roles in the entire life on this world stage and this is the basis of our individual uniqueness. Impressions (Sanskar), being the receptacle of original attributes, virtues, values and all the experiences, project thoughts, desires or feelings on the mind's screen initiating either positive or negative chain of thought and experience depending on the state of soul-consciousness or body-consciousness respectively. A thought, desire or feeling arises in human mind based

on our personality and have molded our characters but which we do not often recognise

our lives. Our present attitudes, beliefs, fears, prejudices and all that gives us a pattern of unconscious or subconscious behaviour have been formed of these events. The negative experiences of the recent past get projected as negative thoughts, desires or feelings frequently because they are at the top of the Stockpile of experiences in the receptacle of   . Even our obsessions, our temper, our lifestyle is because of these. Some of these memories can perhaps be retrieved under special conditions or with the help of hypnotism or drugs. These implicit or latent memories determine in part what we do and

has 5/7th of its mass under water; these unconscious memories form a major part of

on self. All brain-scientists, psychologists and psychiatrists agree that it is this, which

character or personality in man's normal state of wakefulness from moment to moment. In Sanskrit language, these dispositions or unconscious memories, which are the result of previous actions, are called impressions (sanskars). It is these, which give unity to the self. The self coordinates the information received from various senses into various parts of the brain and gives to it an experimental unity without which the encoded memory would be meaningless.

BASIC LAWS OF MEMORY

Registration – Retention – Recollection

There are three stages by which a clear memory is formed. These are Registration, Retention and Recollection.

1. **Registration:** Formation of memory begins with registering the information during

   very limited. At this stage sense organs have to be alert for registering the information clearly. Otherwise, the waste and negative information, which keep coming from subconscious or unconscious memory, might replace it soon.

2. **Retention:** The process of storing the perceived information for longer duration is called Retention. This process involves the third eye's visual imagery, association with words

   in their memory related to that information, or other experiences such as smell or sounds. Periodical revision plan is very necessary for retaining the information for longer duration.

3. **Recollection:**

   is brought up into the conscious mind when it is required. This further depends on the state of mind. Alpha state of mind helps to recall the full information stored in the memory bank.

Working Laws (Operating Laws of Memory)

a. **Law of Belief:** The belief of our mind is the strong impressions of thoughts seen by the two eyes of physical body, visualised by the third eye and experienced it to be true. Belief does not mean faith in some ritual, ceremony, form, and institution or formula; it is simply talking about any belief. All our experiences, events, conditions and acts, which are reproduced

   potential of memory bank to bring about the result.

   A thought is an input in our conscious mind, which acts as memory trigger, or incipient action and the reaction is the response from our memory bank that corresponds to the nature of our thoughts, which entered into our memory bank. Thus our memory bank acts like an ATM machine. As you press the button so is the response from the machine. Fill your bank (ATM Machine) with the concept of harmony, health, peace, goodwill, eternal varieties and truths of life and wonders will happen in your life and you will move

   which has plagued our human kind.

b. **Law of Self-Preservation:** Impressions of natural instincts preserve our physical body by constant renewal processes. In almost eleven month our whole physical body is

   a month, our skeleton in every three months, even the DNA which holds the genetic

material holding memories of millions of Years of evolutionary time undergoes change. The actual raw material of DNA, the carbon, the hydrogen, the nitrogen comes and goes every six weeks like migratory bird. Our physical body we had two years ago is dead and gone and this is the clinching proof of soul's self-preservation and also a proof of a "LIFE AFTER DEATH". We are riding these molecules of body but we are not the molecules we ride. This skin comes and goes every month. It reincarnates once a month, but it does not forget to give the feeling of pleasure and pain. Our stomach cells change

not our physical bodies but we are riding our physical bodies with inbuilt impressions of self-preservation, instincts in our memory bank or subconscious mind which keep functioning automatically without the knowledge of our conscious mind and intellect. The Greek philosopher Herculite has rightly said that you should think of the human body as something like a river. Just like you cannot step into the same river twice because the

out 1022 atoms from everywhere else. And these atoms have their origin in every cells of our body. So at the atomic level we are sharing our organs with each other.

c. **Law of Substitution:** According to the law of substitution, you can activate the impressions of the joy of freedom by your third eye, which can recondition your memory bank. If you have activated the impressions of negative thoughts and conditioned your memory bank negatively, you could also activate the impressions of positive thoughts and recondition your memory positively by the law of substitution of your memory bank. If your third eye took you to wrong habits and stressed life, it now can take you to freedom and peace of mind too. By the law of substitution, you visualise the images of freedom, sobriety and perfection and feel the thrill of accomplishment. When fear knocks the door of the mind, let faith in God and all good things substitute the fear. By the law of substitution only, you can get rid of bad habits and negative thought patterns.

d. **Law of Concentrated Attention or Visualisation:** According to this law the idea or any scene that realises itself is the one to which we give the most concentrated attention or visualise vividly. Due to concentration or more attention on thoughts or ideas by our objective mind, the related impressions of memories get quickly activated and realised in practical life. These are the powerful thoughts or ideas, which are enveloped with the power of emotion to get quickly visualised and realised by our subconscious mind. When you are most attentive, to the idea of failure, it is failure that the subconscious mind brings into reality. The fear of failure itself creates the experience of failure by the law of concentration.

same. Whatever be your mental picture of attention or concentration, your subconscious mind will bring it to happen as per the law of concentration.

e. **Law of Compulsion:** Repeating the thoughts or repeating the acts over in a period of time form active impressions in the memory bank. After that it becomes a second nature

human being gets placed under the compulsion of a habit. This is known as the law of compulsion. If you repeat a negative thought and keep drinking or smoking or doing any bad habits regularly over a period of time, you will place yourself under the compulsion of these negative thoughts and habits. You will have the temptation of doing it automatically according to the law of compulsion. That is why people feel incapable of giving up their bad habits or negative thoughts and emotions, which are hunting their mind with fear, worry and anxiety. The active impressions of bad habits and negative thoughts start interfering the state of mind under the law of compulsion despite our mental effort or mental coercion against the bad habits. This further leads to frustration, depression and mental paranoia. Law of compulsion of Our memory bank makes our destructive habit to operate automatically like Involuntarily actions.

f. **Law of Observation:** If we observe any event or scene with involvement of all sense organs, it gets registered as it is seen. That is why we remember our childhood so vividly. In childhood, there are no negative or waste thoughts, therefore the impressions of childhood remains forever and a child is called the father of the man. With the power of observations we can register anything in our memory for longer duration.

g. **Law of Memory Languages:** As our computer has got programming languages, similarly our human computer has also got unique languages for mind programming. Only these languages get registered in our memory bank. If we want to improve our memory power, we must communicate with our memory bank in these languages only.

Following Four Types of Languages Programme the Mind:

a. **Image:** Image of any things automatically gets impressed in our memory. That is why we recollect the faces of any previously seen person but unable to recollect the name of him.

b. **Music:** Music too gets impressed automatically in our memory, but lyrics doesn't. That is why we feel more relaxed when we listen to music or do msical humming. Alpha music relaxes all muscles and cells of the body.

c. **Colour:** Colour is also the language of mind. That is why colourful things attract our attention and register the impressions of the things in memory. Visualisation of colours not only tunes our inner body (energy body) but also removes the body pains, backache and muscle pain. For that reason only, infrared rays (Heat therapy) are given during Physiotherapy exercise to remove the muscle pain. Visualisation of "Red" colour and pinpointing the energy of red colour to the pain affected region gives more relaxation and relief.

d. **Art:** Art is the creativity of mind, which easily gets impressed in memory. That is why any movie, TV serials or any advertisement (Creative Arts) creates lasting impressions in our memory. Rajyoga meditation is a mental art used for reconditioning and de-conditioning of our memory.

Chapter 2

VARIOUS MEMORY TECHNIQUES:

1. Mnemonics 2. Association 3. Creative visualisation 4. Substitution 5. Alpha techniques

1. Mnemonics

The memory techniques are not a new idea. The ancient Greeks used it extensively. Mnemonics forms a large part of trained memory. The Greeks discovered that human memory is largely an association process that works by linking things together. The main focus while making a mnemonic is to be illogical and humorous as this is easily remembered. The method is to note down all the key ideas or points of the chapter or any question, make a memorable sentence or

words.

Take for example, how we remember the different colours in rainbow: we use a code VIBGYOR for violet, indigo, blue, green, yellow, orange, and red.

A number of people remain skeptical about the potential of human brain, pointing to the substandard performances that many of us routinely churn out. The reason our performances do not match our potential is simply because we are given no information about what we are or about how we can best utilise our inherent qualities. Hence, understanding these basic concepts and techniques of memory will help us to match our performance with our inherent potential.

Mnemonics is named after the Greek Goddess of memory – 'Mnemosyne'. Generally Mnemonics is used to describe the memory techniques which are the basic tools for registration in our memory. It also helps in improving the power of our retention and recollection from our memory. Mnemonics include unusual ways of memorising huge amounts of information.

memory." So we can say that **"Mnemonics is a way of storing the information in the mind by creating an additional interest in it. It makes a deep impression of the information to be memorised in the mind."**

Even in the period of Greeks and Romans, mnemonic techniques are one of the most important subjects taught in classical schools. They were often used by the Great Orators of the time to remember their speeches. Without this technique, their tasks would have been impossible. Mnemonic techniques are not only just a trick, but also a serious method to help us paying attention, registering information, retaining and recalling it from our memory. Since this is a method, we need to practice them over and over in order to become comfortable with using them every day. These techniques do not rely on magic but on our own ability to visualise, making connections or associations and organising important information.

2. Association

Association is a very powerful way of remembering the information. In this system, we hook together the information which we are trying to learn. This is also known as linking system.

We can memorise speeches, articles, points of our subject, shopping list, etc. by linking system. This is also known as 'dominos technique' because as in the domino effect, one event causes a series of similar other events to happen one after the other. In the similar way, we link the words in such a manner that one word causes the next word to happen and so on. It also helps us to remember the series of words easily and effectively.

Take an example of randomily selected words:

Table	Pen	Bomb	Library
Field	Tea	Building	Snakes
Petrol pump	Vegetables	Flag	Leaders
Bridge	Curtains	Market	Cloth mill
Badminton	River		

Have you seen all the objects? Yes! now you can visualise and link them like this:

Now you see this story as colourful as you can in your mind and try the exercise on the next page.

3. Creative Visualisation

Visualisation means giving or creating a mental image of anything. One can visualise anything depending upon one's capability to think, explore without any limitation. Since our memory

understands the language of Art, Image, Colour and Music, visualisation helps a lot in registering any information in our memory, i.e. subconscious mind.

In other words, we can say that visualisation is the technique of using the power of imagination purposefully to focus on a particular topic.

Visualised experience and a real experience have same effect on our mind. **As our subconscious mind or our memory can not differentiate between what is real and what we believe is real. It only receives and registers the impressions of images that are visualised by us and acts or reacts with these images in the same way as it does in real life.**

While visualisation, our simple thought gets enveloped with the power of emotion which further

attention or concentration one's subconscious mind will bring it to happen as per the law of concentration.

Visualisation forces us to concentrate or to pay attention towards any

It develops concentration power.

It improves our long term memory power.

It develops a positive personality.

It plays a great role in Stress management enabling one to lead a tension-free life.

It helps us to learn with fun.

It helps us to develop creativity and inventions.

It helps students to prepare for an examination.

It creates a superior vision.

It provides energy to remove boredom and laziness in life.

It makes our life interesting and optimistic.

4. Substitution

word or idea which we need to memorise is not visual. We cannot imagine abstract ideas or words. To overcome this hurdle, substitution word concept emerges. Substitution word concept can be applied to any seemingly abstract material.

This is also known as PMS-(Personalised Meaning System). In personalised meaning system or substitution, we give a picture to an abstract word by replacing it with a similar sounding 'visual' word. Whenever we need to visualise a particular abstract word we see its personalised meaning. We picture in mind a similar sounding word.

How to do:

Substitution can be used when we hear or see a word that seems abstract or intangible to us.

Whenever we hear or see an intangible word, we should think of something that sounds like or reminds us of that abstract word

Then we should picture it in our mind.

For example:

Generally, the name of person or place can not be pictured in our mind, so we can make their **substitution** as:

Ramanujan – Ram (new) jam   **Italy** – idly (a south Indian dish)

By using a bit of imagination, we can form a conscious association between these two words.

Some more examples of substitution are given below, as they are used in the book:

Lithium – lichee (fruit)   **Hydrogen** – balloon of hydrogen.

Rubidium – ruby (gem)   **Carbon** – car

Pictures, substitute words, thoughts or phrases that we use remind us of the intangible material.

It improves our concentration and makes us remember what we normaly would not do.

5. Alpha Technique

Before knowing one of the best memorising technique lets know in detail "what is alpha wave?" Our mind always generates waves of different frequencies. As described before these waves are of different types. These are:

Type of Wave	Frequency
Beta	14 – 20
Alpha	7-14
Theta	3-7
Delta	½ – 3

Generally at alpha frequency our left brain has great power of logical thinking. As about 10 cycles per second capacity of the brain which is the centre of human intelligence can be increased to a higher degree. At this frequency both left and right hemisphere function together.

Under learning of alpha technique we have to go through four steps:

Step 1: scanning the matter and knowing its essence.

Step 2: high speed reading at alpha.

Step 3: coming back to beta and analysing the matter.

Step 4: returning to alpha for perfect visualisation/feeling.

At alpha frequency our brain receives information very effectively, many times than general period. So at this frequency whatever is read/ learnt, can be remembered easily.

From research it is seen at alpha frequency one can read even 30 times more than the traditional

Remember, it is your eye and brain which take actively for speed reading. Reading loudly slows down the reading speed. So while reading, concentrate your mind on your studies, move the eye speedily and grasp all the study matter at this speed reading. And it is at alpha when the mind is so concentrated that your eyes require less guidance to go through any chapter.

Even our mind is better concentrated and guided if we just start reading 2 to 3 words of a sentence keeping pen/ pencil under the line. After starting with two or three words of a sentence both the eye and brain get their higher speed.

After high speed reading at alpha, when you come back to beta by closing you eyes then all the matter comes before you. Then analyse the matter. and analyse at this beta state (after coming back from alpha) has very powerful result. As in this state your left brain (which is

understanding the whole material. After this again go to alpha state for the most effective retention.

After analysing the matter at beta frequency then come back to alpha again. Now visualise and imagine things properly. Your power of retention depends on how you visualise the matter. Clearer is your visualisation; stronger will be your mental activities. It is because connection between nerves increases with your visualisation & hence your right brain gets highly activated. So your memory increases to a greater degree.

Chapter 3

The best examples of Rhymes (Rhyme Method) ever known are the **Vedas**. Vedas consists of four parts:

1. Samhitas   2. Brahmanas 3. Aranyakas   4. Upanishads

Vedic hymns have typical rhythm. Even though Vedas originated long ago, they passed down the generations orally. Because of their typical rhyme pattern and melody, Vedic hymns have been easily remembered and passed down for generations. Instead of trying to remember

easy to remember them irrespective of the meaningfulness of the new sentence or verse thus formed. The reason for this is the rhythm. The subject you have to study may be dry and boring. You may take out some important words from the lesson with that particular rhythm. Repeat the rhythm a number of times. That's all. You can recall the contents of the lesson by

one or two times. Try to remember at least one or two actual word replacement for gibberish words. Then you automatically remember the whole lesson. By practice you can master this art.

The rhymes method involves every English alphabet and converts them into similar sounding words. See the examples below:

A : Ape	B : Bee	C : Sea
D : Dean	E : Eel	F : Half
G : Jean	H : Itch	I : Eye
J : Jay	K : Cake	L : Hell
M : Ham	N : Hen	O : Hole
P : Pea	Q : Queen	R : Hour
S : Snake	T : Tea	U : Universe
V : Wheel	W : Trouble	X : Eggs
Y : Wine	Z : Zip	

Rhyming Jingles: This is a technique suitable for literature students and also for students who

Comprehensive Memory Development Course

are willing to experiment in academics. A classic example is the nursery rhyme:

Thirty days have September,

April, June and November,

The entire rest has thirty-one

Except February alone.

The technique can be suitably altered to remember those confusing history dates.

Examples:

1. Discovery of America in 1942.
2.
3. Fire of London in 1966.
4.

This is the fast, simplest and effective method of generating mental image. It will help us in

of the number to decide its mental image/code.

Let's start with the number one. One is similar in pronunciation to the word sun or nun or bun, etc. Now we need to select any one of them. Let's select sun. So from now onwards our mental image for one is sun. Similarly think something that rhymes with two. It is essential to make the memory image as imaginative, as colourful and as bright as possible.

For example: For the number 2 we can visualise something similar in pronunciation like *zoo* or s*hoe*. Our mental image for 3 can be *tree* or k   .

One	-	Sun
Two	-	Shoe/Zoo
Three	-	Tree
Four	-	Door
Five	-	Wife/Knife
Six	-	Kicks/ Vicks
Seven	-	Heaven
Eight	-	Plate/Slate
Nine	-	Wine
Ten	-	Hen/Den
Eleven	-	Lemon
Twelve	-	Shelve
Thirteen	-	Thirsting (visualise a thirsty Man with a glass of water)

Fourteen	-	Fort in (entering into a big fort)
Fifteen	-	Lifting (weight lifter)
Sixteen	-	Sweet sixteen (a beautiful girl)
Seventeen	-	Seth in (a fat seth)
Eighteen	-	Attacking (scene of a war)
Nineteen	-	Namkeen
Twenty	-	Aunty (your favourite aunty)

Take the problem of the shopping list. You already know what usually happens when you have to shop a llist of items. Before leaving for shopping you continue writing down what you need.

troubles. Make up your list as you go along, and retain it in your head.

For the sake of practice let us take a fairly typical shopping list and see how the items may be

1. Shirt 2. Ball 3. Calculator 4. Knife 5. Cake 6. Pepsi 7. Football 8. Soap 9. DDT

Let's try to memorise the items with the help of memory codes.

RHYME METHOD CODES

1 Sun		11 Lemon	
2 Shoe		12 Shelf	
3 Tree		13 Thirsting	
4 Door		14 Fort-in	
5 Knife		15 Lifting	
6 Kicks		16 Sweet sixteen	
7 Heaven		17 Seth (in)	
8 Plate		18 Attacking	
9 Wine		19 Namkeen	
10 Hen		20 Aunty	

IGFA Neurobic Gym

Comprehensive Memory Development Course

1. **Sun with shirt:** Visualise your wet shirt is drying in the sunlight.
2. **Ball with shoe:** You are unable to wear a shoe since balls are inside.
3. **Calculator with tree:** A tree on which a lot of calculators are hanging.
4. **Knife with door:** Unable to open the door, so cutting with a knife.
5. **Cake with wife:** Offering cake to wife on her birthday.
6. **Pepsi with Vicks:** Angry at the shopkeeper when you got the taste of Vicks from the Pepsi.
7. **Football with heaven:** You hit the ball so hard that it went to heaven.
8. **Soap with plate:** Applying soap on plate to clean it.
9. **DDT with wine:** Dissolving DDT in wine to purify it.
10. **Stapler with hen:** Stapling hen's beak so that it may not disturb you by cocking.
11. **Watch with lemon:** After peeling off the lemon you got a watch inside.
12.
    them.
13. **Potato with thirsting:** Eating potato dish and drinking lots of water.
14. **Rubber with fort in:** Sweeper cleaning the wall of fort with rubber.
15. **Mirror with lifting:** A weightlifter is lifting a heavy mirror.

When you visualise according to the above-mentioned way, you have prepared a list of items, which you want to buy from market. Now you can easily recall the items serially and can buy all the items without missing anyone of them.

We will discuss to learn the history dates in the next chapters.

Chapter 4

Shape Method

For learning more codes we can take the help of shape method. More codes mean more mental racks to store data in our memory. We will create Shape Code for 1 to 20 as follows:

1. Stick (One looks like a stick)
2. Duck (we can make a duck with digit 2)

1	1	| Stick	**11**		|| Road
2	2	Duck	**12**	12	Cap
3	3	Heart	**13**	13	Butterfly
4	4	Chair	**14**	4	Boat
5	5	Hook	**15**	15	Cigar
6	6	Hockey stick	**16**	16	Elephant trunk
7	7	Lamppost	**17**	17	Sandwich
8	8	Spectacle	**18**	18	Suntimer
9	9	Lollypop	**19**	19	Compass
10	10	Bat ball	**20**	20	Scooter

3. Heart/Om (we can make a symbol of heart or Om by digit 3)
4. Chair (looks like a chair)
5. Hook (Looks like a hook)
6. Hockey stick (Looks like a hockey stick)
7. Lamp post (Looks like a lamp post)
8. Spectacles (We can make a shape of spectacle with 8)
9. Lolly pop (Looks like a lolly pop)
10. Bat and ball (Looks like a bat and ball)
11. Road/Legs/wickets (Looks like two legs) or plain road
12. Door knob (We can make a picture of a door knob with 1 and 2)

15. Cigar/Sitar (We can make a shape of sitar with or cigar 1 and 5)
16. Elephant's trunk (We can make a shape of an elephant trunk by using 1 and 6)
17. Sandwich/Bread Pakauda (We can make a triangular bread   or sandwich by joining 1 & 7)
18. Suntimer/Binocular (We can make a shape of a binocular or suntimer with digit1 and 8)
19. Nailcutter/Nut Cracker (We can make a shape of a nut cracker or Nailcutter by joining 1 and 9)
20. Scooter (We can make a shape of an old scooter by digit 2 and 0)

Chapter 5

As it is clear by its name that it is related to some value of the words or idea which we are trying to remember. In this system, we imagine the value of a number to give it a picture. We can do it as follows:

One: One means a single entity. So we can give the picture or image to 'One' as with 'Prime Minister' or 'President' or 'Raja' of a country. So in value system, we can imagine one as 'Raja' or 'King'.

Similarly, we can convert other numbers into images as under:

Number	Mental Image
1.	Raja
2.	Couple
3.	Three Monkeys of Gandhiji
4.	Four wheeler vehicle
5.	Pandavas in Mahabharat
6.	Sixer of Sachin Tendulkar
7.	Seven Colour of Rainbow
8.	Octopus
9.	Nine Planets
10.	Ten heads of Ravan in Ramanyan
11.	Football or cricket team
12.	One dozen banana
13.	A horrible event as 13 considered as unlucky number
14.	Ram's exile to jungle for 14 years.
15.	Independence Day, 15th August.
16.	A sweet sixteen girl or beautiful teenager girl.
17.	7 Up (cold drink) in tin

18.	Voter's age
19.	1900 century, your birthday.
20.	Lottery ticket of Rs. 20 lakh.

Chapter 6

Each one of us comes across many numbers in a day. It may be a telephone number, a date, a bank account number, vehicle number, mathematics calculations, formulae, house numbers or a long series of numbers, and so on.

21 32 10 83 63 45 91 03 08 13 73 46 86 11 09 51 75 50 10 ……..

But the question is how to memorise the numbers, as they are the abstract forms of information. Although they are visible and have an image or a particular picture even then you are unable to memorise them.Things become terrible if you are a political science, law, or commerce student where you have to memorise articles and sections or sub-sections of various laws. Many students mug them up just to forget them at the time of examination or interview. This becomes a scary problem when you get stuck at the very beginning of your paper because there is a huge pressure and you are bound to forget whatever you might have been able to retain or recall during the rest of your exam. We have devised a simple method to deal with numbers and memorise them with ease. This is called PHONETIC METHOD. Phonetic method helps

alphabets that can be formed into words for which you already have a picture dictionary in your mind. The sequence of these alphabets is as under.

Number	Alphabet	Explanation
1.	t or d	small "t" or "d" has one down stroke
2.	n	small "n"requires two down strokes or the shape of n is similar to 2
3.	m	"m" requires three down strokes or the shape of m is similar to 3
4.	r	four in majority of languages ends with "r". In hindi, it's , in latin it's quarter, in Russian its shutter, etc.
5.	l	In Roman "L" means 50, here small "l" means 5
6.	j or g	The mirror image of "j" is like 6.
	Ch or sh	The reverse of "g" is like 6. Hindi pronunciation of 6, sound like or .
7.	k	Two sevens can form a "k".

8.	f or v	The shape of small "f"
9.	P or b	They both look like mirror image and inverted image of 9.
10.	S, Z	"Z"

Phonetic Method helps us in various ways to memorise. It also helps us to memorise any information that has numbers in it, one by one. But before that I would like to give you some more codes, pertaining to the memory method, to help you learn the calendar of 500 years.

Let us make the codes of 1 to 100 with pictures through this phonetic method:

0.	Sea	
1.	Tie	
2.	Eno	
3.	Maa	
4.	Ray	
5.	Hall	
6.	Jaw	
7.	Key	
8.	Fee	
9.	Bee	
10.	DoSa	

11.	DaDa (In Cricket)	
12.	DeN	
13.	DaM	
14.	DeeR	
15.	Doll	
16.	TaJ	
17.	Teeka	
18.	T.V.	
19.	TaP	
20.	NaSa	

21.	NeT	
22.	NuN	
23.	NeeM	
24.	NeeR	
25.	NaiL	
26.	NaCH (Dance)	
27.	NecK	
28.	NaVy	
29.	NiB (Imagine an inky nib)	
30.	MeSs	

31.	MaT	
32.	MooN	
33.	MaMa	
34.	Mira	
35.	MaiL	
36.	MatCH	
37.	MiKe	
38.	Movie	
39.	MaP	
40.	RoSe	

41.	RaT	
42.	RaiN	
43.	RaM	
44.	RoaR or Rear (mirror)	
45.	RaiL	
46.	RaJa	
47.	RacK	
48.	RooF	
49.	RoPe	
50.	LaSe (Lace, 'C' pronounced as 'S')	

51.	LoTa	
52.	Lion	
53.	LiMe	
54.	LawyeR	
55.	Laloo	
56.	Lichi	
57.	LaKe	
58.	LeaF	
59.	LaB	
60.	CHeSs	

61.	Jet	
62.	CHaiN	
63.	JaM	
64.	JaR	
65.	JaiL	
66.	Jug	
67.	JacK	
68.	CHeF or chief	
69.	Jeep	
70.	CaSe	

71.	Kite	
72.	Gun	
73.	Gum	
74.	CaR	
75.	CoaL	
76.	CaSH	
77.	CaKe	
78.	Coffee	
79.	CaP	
80.	FuSe	

Comprehensive Memory Development Course

81.	FooT	
82.	FaN	
83.	FM	
84.	FiRe	
85.	FiLe	
86.	FiSH	
87.	ForK	
88.	Fifa	
89.	ViP (Suitcase)	
90.	BuS	

91.	Pot	
92.	Pen	
93.	PM	
94.	Bear	
95.	BelL	
96.	Beach	
97.	BiKe	
98.	BuFfet (Pronounced as Bufe)	
99.	BaBy	
100.	Dices	

Now, let us try to make the codes form 101 to 1000:		
101.	TeST	
102.	TSN (the sports network)	
103.	TeaSe Me	
104.	DuSeRah	
105.	TuSseL	
106.	DiScharGe	
107.	DeSK	
108.	DoZe ofF	
109.	DSP (Deputy Suprintendent of Police)	
110.	TaDdieS (Toys)	

111.	DaD-Dad (Baby talk)	
112.	TiTaN	
113.	DaTe hiM (His clothes date him)	
114.	TarTaRe (Sauce)	
115.	TiDaL (river)	
116.	DoTaGe (Parent looks at child)	
117.	Too ThicK (People choosing not to go out in fog)	
118.	TooTh oF (Holding up a tooth of an animal)	
119.	DTP (DeskTop Publishing)	
120.	TeNniS	

121.	TeNT	
122.	TaNNing (On a sun bed)	
123.	DeNiM (Shirt)	
124.	DiNner (singer)	
125.	TuNneL	
126.	TiN edge (Rough edge of a tin) or Teenage	
127.	TaNK	
128.	TurN ofF (Switching off the radio)	
129.	DuNloP	
130.	DMS (Delhi Milk Scheme)	

131.	DaMaD (Son-in-law)	
132.	TaMaNa (wish)	
133.	DuMMy	
134.	TaMeR (Lion tamer)	
135.	TaMiL	
136.	TaMaCHa (Guerilla soldier in Sri Lanka)	
137.	DMK (party)	
138.	TiMe ofF (Person relaxing at home)	
139.	DaMP (Pipe smoker tamping down tobacco)	
140.	TeaRS	

141.	TaRT	
142.	TaRuN (a friend)	
143.	TeRM (School term)	
144.	Ta Ra Ra (Panjabi goodbye)	
145.	TRiaL	
146.	ToRCH	
147.	TRacK (Railway)	
148.	TRofFy	
149.	DRoP	
150.	TaiLS	

151.	DeLTa	
152.	Two LaNe	
153.	TaaLeeM	
154.	TaiLoR	
155.	DoLL	
156.	Talash	
157.	TiLak	
158.		
159.	TuLiP	
160.	TiSsueS	

161.	T-SHirT	
162.	Two CHiNs (Double chinned person)	
163.	TouCH Me	
164.	TeaCHeR	
165.	DeJaL	
166.	To CHurCH (Signpost pointing to a church)	
167.	Two CHeQues	
168.	To SHaVe (Person going to the bathroom to shave)	
169.	The SHiP (Name on a pub)	
170.	Tie CaSe (Cloth, or cardboard, case for ties)	

171.	Two CaTs or TicKeT	
172.	ToKeN	
173.	Two CoMbs	
174.	TucKeR (Tucker bag)	
175.	TacKLe (Fishing tackle)	
176.	DiKSHa	
177.	Tea CaKe	
178.	TaKe ofF (Aeroplane taking off)	
179.	TaKe uP (Slowly taking up the slack of a low rope)	
180.	ToFfeeS	

181.	Two FeeT	
182.	DaFaN	
183.	Two FarMs	
184.	Two FaiRies	
185.	ToFeL (exams)	
186.	Two FiSH	
187.	Two ForK	
188.		
189.	Two ViP (Suitcase)	
190.	TaPS (Basin or bath taps)	

191.	DPT (Injection to the children)	
192.	DarPaN	
193.	Tea- PM (having tea with Prime minister)	
194.	TaPeR Cannon lighter	
195.	DimPLe Dimple Kapadi	
196.	Two BuSH	
197.	Two BooK	
198.	Two Bees	
199.	Two PiPe	
200.	NSS	

Comprehensive Memory Development Course

201.	NeST	
202.	NisSaN car	
203.	NaSeeM	
204.	NaZaR (Eyes)	
205.	NaSaL (Speaking with a cold, or spraying a nasal spray)	
206.	No SaSH (Man in a dress suit holding his trousers up because he has no sash)	
207.	No SocK (Person with one bare foot)	
208.	NoSe ofF (Person having his/ her nose cut off)	
209.	KNeeS uP (a dance)	
210.	NeTS	

211.	NTT (Nursery Teacher Training)	
212.	NiTiN	
213.	NaDeeM	
214.	NaDiRa (Heroine)	
215.	No TaiL (Guinea pig)	
216.	NoTCH	
217.	NaTaK	
218.	NaTiVe	
219.	New TaP (Replacing a tap on a bath or sink)	
220.	NuNS	

221.	NaNDa (Heroine)	
222.	Na Na Na (re) (Delar Mehandi)	
223.	NaNa Maa (Your Nana & your mother)	
224.	NiNe Ray	
225.		
226.	NiNJa	
227.	No NecK (Person without a neck)	
228.	New NaV	
229.	No NiB	
230.	NaMeS (nameplate)	

231.	NaMasTe	
232.	No MaN (A land where there is no man)	
233.	New MuM (Someone being introduced to their father's new wife)	
234.	NuMbeR	
235.	NorMaL (An ideal family with 2 children)	
236.	No MatCH (A large and a small boxer in the ring together)	
237.	NaMaK (Salt)	
238.	NoMinatiVe	
239.	New MoP (Putting a new mop head on a handle)	
240.	NuRSe	

241.	NaRaD	
242.	New RuN	
243.	No RooM (No room's sign at a guesthouse)	
244.	No RoaR (Lion who cannot roar)	
245.	NaRiaL (Coconut)	
246.	NouRiSH (A mother feeding a child)	
247.	NewYoRK	
248.	NeRVe	
249.	No RoPe	
250.	NaiLS (Tin or box of nails)	

251.	NaiLeD	
252.	NyLoN	
253.	No LaMb (Sign outside a butcher's ship saying no lamb)	
254.	New LorRy (Shiny new lorry)	
255.	New LaLoo (Give a new look to Laloo)	
256.	KNowLedGe	
257.	New LocK (Someone changing the door lock)	
258.	NulLiFy / New LoVe	
259.	No LiP (Person with no lower lip)	
260.	New SHoeS	

261.	New SHirT	
262.	No WaSHiNg (Empty laundry basket)	
263.	No SHaMe (Drunk behaving badly)	
264.	No CHaiR Table without Chair	
265.	NiGhaL (To Swallow)	
266.	No SHeSHa	
267.	cheques left)	
268.	UnSHaVen	
269.		
270.	NecKS	

271.	NaKeD	
272.	No KaN (Person without ear)	
273.	New CoMb (Someone buying a new comb)	
274.	NauKaR (Servant)	
275.	NucKLe (cheating / copy)	
276.	No CaSH someone turning their pockets inside out	
277.	No KuKoo (Bird)	
278.	New CofFee (Popping the seal on a new jar of instant coffee)	
279.	NaKaB	
280.	New FuSe	

Comprehensive Memory Development Course

281.	No FeeT (Person without feet)	
282.	No FuN	
283.	No FilM (See Cinema Hall)	
284.	No FuR (Mangy dog)	
285.	NoVeL	
286.		
287.	INVoKe (Calling up a spirit, or citing a law or regulation)	
288.	New ViVa (girl)	
289.	ENFeeBle (To make weak)	
290.	NeePS (Scots for turnips)	

291.	New PeT (A family playing with a new puppy)	
292.	NipPoN (A killer-trade name)	
293.		
294.	NiPpeR (baby)	
295.	NePaL (Image of Mount Everest and monks)	
296.	New PaGe (Sometime writing and starting a new page)	
297.		
298.	NewsPaper Vala	
299.	NiPPo (Battery)	
300.	MoSS	

301.	MiST	
302.	MaSoN	
303.	MuSeuM	
304.	MiSeR	
305.	MiSsiLe	
306.	MaSsaGe	
307.	MuSiC	
308.		
309.	MaSh uP	
310.	MaTS (Set of table mats)	

311.	MaTT Not glossy	
312.	MuTtoN	
313.	MaDaM	
314.	MeTeR (Parking meter)	
315.	MeTaL (Lump of iron)	
316.	MiTiGate	
317.	MaTaKa (Mud Pot	
318.	MoTiF (A badge on the front of a car)	
319.	MuD Pie	
320.	MaNSi / MaNaS	

Comprehensive Memory Development Course

321.	MiNT	
322.	MorNiNg (Sun rising)	
323.	MiNiM (Musical symbol)	
324.	MiNoR (Morris Minor)	
325.	MaNiLa (Writing paper of a brownish shade)	
326.	MaNoJ	
327.	MoNKey / MoNK	
328.	My NaVy	
329.	MaNiPlant	
330.	MiMeS (Several people doing mimes)	

331.	MiMeTic	
332.	More MoNey	
333.	My MoM	
334.	MurMuR	
335.	MaMmaL	
336.	My MatCH (Winning a tennis match)	
337.	My MiKe (See yourself holding a mike)	
338.	MuMmFy	
339.	MuMP (A neck swollen on one side)	
340.	MaRS	

341.	MaRT (Cattle market)	
342.	MaRiNe	
343.	MaRry Me (Someone down on one knee proposing marriage)	
344.	MirRoR	
345.	MiRacLe	
346.	MaRriaGe (Pair of wedding rings)	
347.	MaRK (Dirty mark on clean garment)	
348.	MRF Tyres	
349.	MuRadaBad (Brass ware famous)	
350.	MiLlS (Lancashire mills with smoke pouring from chimneys)	

351.	MoLD / MeLT	
352.	MiLaN	
353.	MuLayaM (singh yadav)	
354.	MoLaR (Back tooth)	
355.	MaLL	
356.	MiLeaGe (Speedmeter in a car)	
357.	MiLK	
358.	MoLtoVa	
359.	MaiLBag	
360.	MaCHiS (Match box)	

361.	MidGeT (Dwarf, or MG midget)	
362.	MaCHiNe	
363.	MuSHrooM	
364.	MaJoR (High-ranking soldier)	
365.	My SHelL (Crab pointing to his shell and telling you it is his)	
366.	MaGGi	
367.	MaGiC (Conjurer with wand stick)	
368.	MatCH Fair (Imagine a fair where different kinds of matches are sold)	
369.	My CHaP (Lady pointing to her partner and saying 'this is my chap')	
370.	MaSKS	

371.	MarKeT	
372.	MaKaN (Home)	
373.	MarK Man (A man putting mark on houses)	
374.	My CaR (Your car)	
375.	MiChaeL (Jackson)	
376.	My CaSH (Taking cash out of your pocket and looking at it)	
377.	My CaKe (Your birthday cake)	
378.	My CaVe (Someone pointing to a cave where he or she lived)	
379.	MaKe uP	
380.	MoVieS	

381.	MuFfeT (miss)	
382.		
383.		
384.	My FaiR (You owning a fair)	
385.	MarVeL (Dried milk)	
386.	My FiSH (Someone pointing to their aquarium)	
387.	My FolK (Your family group)	
388.	My FaV (My favourite)	
389.	MoVe uP Someone climbing a ladder	
390.	MaPS	

Phonetic Method

391.	MoPeD	
392.	My BiN Several dustbins outside houses, one with your initials	
393.	My BoMb	
394.	EmPiRe	
395.	MaPLe Syrup	
396.	AmBuSH	
397.	My BooK	
398.	MoP oFfer (Special offer on mops in a shop)	
399.	IMBiBE	
400.	RSS (Rastriya Swyam Sewak Sangh)	

401.	RuST	
402.	RaiSiN	
403.	ReSuMe (Summing up main points in a speech or lecture)	
404.	RaZoR	
405.	RuSseL	
406.	RuSGulla	
407.	RuSK	
408.	ReSerVe	
409.	ReCiePe	
410.	RiTeS (last)	

Phonetic Method

411.	RoTaTe	
412.	RoTteN (Apples, for example)	
413.	ReaDy Me	
414.	WRiTeR (Person with a pen)	
415.	ReTicuLar / RaTtLe	
416.	RaDiSH	
417.	HRiTiK (Hritik Roshan)	
418.	WRiTe oFf (Crashed car)	
419.	WRiTe uP (Report of research, for example)	
420.	RuNS (cricket)	

421.	ReNT	
422.	RaiN iN (Rain water coming through ceiling)	
423.	URaNiuM	
424.	RuNneR (marathon)	
425.	RuNneL (gutter)	
426.	RaNGe (shooting range)	
427.	RiNK (ice)	
428.	RaiN oFf (Cricket or tennis match stopped due to rain)	
429.	RuN uP (Pre election campaign)	
430.	RooMS	

431.	ReMaDe (Remade bed)	
432.	RoMaN (Soldier)	
433.	RiMMan	
434.	RuMouR (Someone whispering behind someone else's back)	
435.	Ram Manohar Lohia (Hospital)	
436.	RaManuJ	
437.	ReMaKe (Tailor remaking a suit)	
438.	ReMoVe (Trouble maker being removed from a club)	
439.	RaMP	
440.	RoaRS (Several lions roaring)	

441.	R eaReaD	
442.	RaRe oNe (Large diamond)	
443.	WaR RooM (Room where war strategies are planned)	
444.	Raw RecRuit (Soldiers protesting their lack of experience to carry out adangerous attack)	
445.	RuRaL (Country image)	
446.	Rare RaSH	
447.	RouRKela	
448.	RameshwaR Farm (Rameshwar Temple & farming is going on outside Temple)	
449.	ReseRve Bank	
450.	RaiLS (For railway engines)	

451.	RouLetTe	
452.	HaiR LoaN / RoLoN (leading some hair to someone who is bald)	
453.	ReaLM (area)	
454.	RolLeR (Instruments)	
455.	RaiL wheel (Train wheel)	
456.	ReLiSH	
457.	ReLocK	
458.	ReLieF (Famine relief food parcels being dropped by Helicopter)	
459.	RolL uP (Hand rolled cigarette)	
460.	RuSHeS	

461.	RaCHiT	
462.	RoSHaN (Rakesh Roshan)	
463.	RaSHMi	
464.	RiCHeR (Some rich person like Amitabh Bachhan)	
465.	RuSH hill (Hillside covered with rushes)	
466.	Re-JudGe (Judge something again)	
467.	Raw CHeeK (Someone's cheeks red with cold)	
468.	RuSH ofF (Somebody rushing off to catch train)	
469.	RiSHaBh	
470.	RacKS (For wine)	

471.	RacKeT	
472.	R.K. Narayanan (Ex. President)	
473.	RaKam (Money)	
474.	RocKeR	
475.	RasCaL	
476.	RicKSHaw	
477.	Raw CaKe (Eating cake that is not cooked)	
478.	ReCoVery	
479.	RaKaB (Ganj) Gurudwara	
480.	RooFS	

481.	RaFT	
482.	RaVeeNa (Tandon)	
483.	ReVaMp (Renovate or liven up)	
484.	RiVeR	
485.	RaVeL (Parvesh Rawal)	
486.	RaVaGe	
487.	ReVoKe (Take away a right)	
488.	ReViVe	
489.	RaVe uP	
490.	RiBS	

491.	RoPeD (Roped off scene of crime, or dangerous area)	
492.	RiPoN (Horse races)	
493.	RoPe Making	
494.	RuBbeR	
495.	RipPLe	
496.	RuBbiSH	
497.	ReBuKe (Someone giving a reprimand)	
498.	RiP oFf / RPF (Complaining about the cost of a meal)	
499.	RiP uP (Person ripping up paper)	
500.	LoSS	

501.	LiST	
502.	LooSeN (Someone loosening their belt, perhaps after a meal)	
503.	Last SuM	
504.	LaSeR	
505.	Lee SaLe	
506.	LaZiz CHai	
507.	LuSaKa (Capital of Zambia)	
508.	LaZaVab (Resturant)	
509.	Low SlaB	
510.	LoTS (Draw lots)	

511.	LooTeD (Shop with broken window and goods scattered by escaping thieves)	
512.	LonDoN	
513.	LeaD arM (Someone with a lead arm)	
514.	LighTeR	
515.	LitTLe	
516.	OLD aGe	
517.	LaTaK	
518.	LaTiFa	
519.	LighT uP	
520.	LaNeS (In the road)	

521.	LiNneT / Lower NeT (bird)	
522.	LiNeN	
523.	LoaN Man	
524.	LoNeR (Person drinking alone at a bar)	
525.	'L' shaped NaiL	
526.	LuNCH	
527.	LiNK (Chain link)	
528.	LoNgeVity (Five lame men)	
529.	LiNe uP	
530.	LiMeS (Tree full of them)	

Phonetic Method

531.	LiMiT (Speed limit sign)	
532.	LeMoN	
533.	LaMe Mare	
534.	LuMbeR	
535.	LiMe aLe (Drink made with lime)	
536.	EeL MatCH (Someone matching pairs of eels for size)	
537.	OiLy MarK	
538.	Low MoVe	
539.	Low Mob	
540.	LRS (Left-Right Side)	

541.	LoRD	
542.	LeaRN (pupil in school)	
543.	LaRa & Me	
544.	LoRRy	
545.	LauReL	
546.	OiLs RuSH (Rush of prospectors to area rumoured' to have oil)	
547.	LaRK	
548.	LaRVa	
549.	OiLy RoPe	
550.	LiLieS	

551.	OiL LighT (On dashboard of car)	
552.	Ley LiNe	
553.	LaLiMa (early morning sun rays)	
554.	OiL LoRry (Oil tanker)	
555.	Low LoLly (Ice lolly almost sucked to nothing)	
556.	Low LatCH (On door so low you have to sit down to it)	
557.	LaLKar	
558.	Low LiFe	
559.	Lower LiP	
560.	LiCHiS	

561.	Low JeT	
562.	LeGioN	
563.	LodGe Me (Standing in a Lodge)	
564.	LodGeR	
565.	Oil SHaLe	
566.	ALl JewiSH	
567.	LoGiK	Logik
568.	OiLy SHaVe (Shaving with motor oil instead of shaving foam)	
569.	OiL SHiP (tanker)	
570.	LaKeS	

571.	LocKeT	
572.	LaKhaN (Anil Kapoor)	
573.	LaKMe (cream)	
574.	LocKeR	
575.	LoCaL (pub)	
576.	LaKSHay	
577.	Low KicK (Football kick low into the goal)	
578.	Low CaVe (Cave below sea level)	
579.	LocK uP (Garage or shop)	
580.	LeaVeS	

581.	LiFT	
582.	LaFuNder	
583.	Low F.M. (Slow down FM radio)	
584.	LiVeR (organ)	
585.	LoVeLy (beautiful)	
586.	OiLy FiSH (Herring, mackerel, trout)	
587.		
588.	LeaF ofF (Leaf off a rubber plant laying besides it)	
589.	LiFeBoy	
590.	LiPS	

591.	LiliPuT	
592.	LiPtoN (Tea)	
593.	Low BeaM (Dipped headlights)	
594.	LeoPaRd	
595.	LaBeL	
596.	LaPCHas (Tribes)	
597.	LaPaK	
598.	LeaP ofF (Leaping off cliff)	
599.	LaP uP (Cat drinking saucer of milk)	
600.	CHeeSeS	

601.	CHeST	
602.	JohnSoN (& Johnson)	
603.	CHaSe Me (Child or dog playing tag)	
604.	CHaSeR (Whisky with a pint of beer)	
605.	GaSLine	
606.	JasSi SHow	
607.	CHuSKi (ice candy)	
608.	Jackie ShroFf	
609.	CheeSe Pie (A pie made of cheese)	
610.	SHaDeS (sunglasses)	

Phonetic Method

611.	SHuTT	
612.	CHeaTiNg	
613.	SHowTiMe (Actors getting ready for show)	
614.	SHooTeR (gun)	
615.	SHuTtLe (Euro-star or space shuttle)	
616.	CHaT SHow	
617.	SHeD Key	
618.	SHuT ofF (Turning the water off)	
619.	CHaT uP (Chatting up with the member of opposite sex)	
620.	CHiNS	

621.	SHaNTi	
622.	JiNN	
623.	SHow NaMe (plate) (People having name badges checked as they enter aconference hall)	
624.	SHiNneR (Black eye)	
625.	SHaNeL (Cloth)	
626.	CHaNGe (coins)	
627.	CHuNK	
628.	GeNeVa	
629.	CHiN uP (Person holding his chin up to give him courage)	
630.	CHarMiS (Cream)	

631.	ASHaMeD (Person bowing their head in shame)	
632.	SHow MaN	
633.	SHaMMy (Kapoor)	
634.	SHow MaRe (Prize mare at a show)	
635.	SHow MiLes (speedometer)	
636.	SHoe MatCH (Shoe sale with attendants trying to match odd shoes)	
637.	ShaMaK (Dawar)	
638.	GMF (General Manager Finance)	
639.	JuMP	
640.	SHaReS	

641.	SHiRT	
642.	JouRNey	A HAPPY JOURNEY
643.	CHaiR arM	
644.	CHandeR chuR	
645.	CHaRLie (Charlie Chapplin)	
646.	ChaRGe	positive charge negative charge
647.	SHaRK	
648.	CHaRVi	Charvi Diamonds
649.	CHiRP (Bird chirping)	
650.	SHelLS (Sea)	

651.	SHieLD	
652.	SHelLiN(g) (In war)	
653.	JaL Mahal	
654.	JeweLleR	
655.	SHelL oiL (Sign on service station)	
656.	SHaLJa	
657.	CHaLK	
658.	SHeLF	
659.	ChiLsi Pie (Hot spicy pie)	
660.	JudGeS	

Comprehensive Memory Development Course

661.	JudGemenT	
662.	JaSHaN (Celebration)	
663.	ASH JaM (Jam made of ash and everyone retching after eating it)	
664.	CHeSHieR	
665.	CHurCHiL	
666.	CHew JudGe (Chewing up a judge)	
667.	CHurCHS Key (Massive key)	
668.	JudGe Fee (Judge being paid fee)	
669.	SHoe SHoP	
670.	CHecKS	

671.	JacKeT	
672.	CHicKeN	
673.	CHeck me	
674.	CHoKeR / JoKeR	
675.	CHucKLe	
676.	SHare KaJu	
677.	CHucKKey (Floor mill)	
678.	JacK Fruit	
679.	CHecK uP (Medical check up)	
680.	SHaFtS	

Comprehensive Memory Development Course

681.	CHafFeD	
682.	SHaVeN	
683.	SHaVe Me (Sitting in barber's chair and asking the barber to shave you)	
684.	SHaVeR (electric)	
685.	SHoVeL	
686.		
687.	JFK (President Kennedy)	
688.	CHaVVi	
689.	GiVe uP	
690.	CHiPS	

691.	CHipPeD	
692.	SHopPiNg	
693.	SHow PoeM	The Reason Why
694.	CHoPpeR	
695.	CHaPeL	
696.	SHeePiSH	
697.	SHoP Key (Someone taking out key to open shop)	
698.	CHoP oFf (Tree branch)	
699.		
700.	CaSeS	

701.	CaSetTe	
702.	CaSiNo	
703.	KiSs Me	
704.	KaiSeR (German Emperor)	
705.	CaStLe	
706.	Cow SearCH (Villagers searching for lost cow)	
707.	CoSkeT	
708.	KeSaV	
709.	CuSP (Point at which two curves meet)	
710.	CaTS	

711.	KiTTy (party)	
712.	KiTteN	
713.	CaDiuM	
714.	CaTeR (To give)	
715.	CaTtLe	
716.	CoTtaGe	
717.	CuTtacK	
718.	CuT ofF	
719.	CoT uP (Cot upside down)	
720.	CaNS	

Comprehensive Memory Development Course

721.	CaNT (Delhi Cantt.)	
722.	CaNnoN	
723.	CaN of aaM (Can full of aam (Mangoes)	
724.	CorNeR	
725.	CaNaL	
726.	KiNG	
727.	KaNnaK (Gold)	
728.	CoNVoy	
729.	CaNoPy	
730.	CoMbS	

731.	CoMeT	
732.	ComMoN (Common person or common piece of ground)	
733.	Come MoM (calling mother)	
734.	CaMeRa	
735.	CaMeL	
736.	KaMCHor (See a person)	
737.	CoMiC	
738.	CoMFort (Inn)	
739.	CaMP	
740.	CaRS	

741.	CaRT	
742.	CoRN	
743.	CRuM(b)	
744.	KaRaRe (crisp)	
745.	CoRaL	
746.	CRaSH	
747.	CRacK	
748.	CuRVe	
749.	CRoP	
750.	CLasS	

751.	CLoT	Blood Clot Diagram
752.	CLaN (Represented by tartan)	
753.	CaLM (Calm sea)	
754.	CLeaR (Empty road)	
755.	KiLL	
756.	ColLaGe	
757.	CLocK	
758.	CLifF	
759.	CLiP (Paper clip)	
760.	CatCHeS (Catches in cricket)	

Comprehensive Memory Development Course

761.	CaGeD	
762.	KitCHeN	
763.	KariSHMa	
764.	CatCHeR (Rat catcher)	
765.	CudGeL	
766.	KaGaJ (paper)	
767.	Cat CHoC (Chocolate cat)	
768.	KeSHaV	
769.	KatCHuP/ KaSHyaP	
770.	CorKS	

771.	CooKeD/ KaKDi	
772.	CoCooN	
773.	CuCuMber	
774.	CooKeR	
775.	CacKLe (Of hens)	
776.	KaKaJi	
777.	Kis-2-ki Kismat (movie)	
778.	Cow CaVe (Cave where cows sleep)	
779.	KicK uP (football)	
780.	CaFeS (Many coffee shops)	

781.	CaVeaT (Legal warning)	red flag caveat emptor
782.		
783.	CaVeMan	
784.	CaVeR	
785.	CaVvaLee (Song)	
786.	KaVaCH (Armour)	
787.	CaVe Key (Map of cave systems)	
788.	Cry ViVa (People at celebration crying Viva-meaning long life)	
789.	CraVe uP (Road abuse)	
790.	CaPeS	

791.	CarPeT	
792.	CouPoN	
793.	Cow PoeM (Poem about cows)	
794.	CoPpeR	
795.	CaBLe	
796.	CaBbaGe	
797.	KoPecK (Russian coin)	
798.	CaP ofF (Someone taking cap off)	
799.	CoBweB	
800.	FaCeS	

Comprehensive Memory Development Course

801.	FaST	
802.	FiSsioN (Nuclear power station)	
803.	FiSH Meal	
804.	FiSsuRe	
805.	FaCiaL (Woman being given facial beauty creams)	
806.	ViSaGe (Stern face)	
807.	VaSCo (explorer)	
808.	WaVe SaVe (Estuary barrier for harnessing wave energy to make electricity)	
809.	FuSeD (Blackened electric bulb indicating that it is fused)	
810.	FaTS (Meat fat, together with potatoes on plate)	

811.	FaDeD (Faded jeans)	
812.	FatTeN (Cow or pig)	
813.	FaThoM	
814.	WaTeR	
815.	FaTaL (Dead person)	
816.	FooTaGe (newsprint)	
817.	VoDKa	
818.	Fix Deposit Fund	
819.	FeeT uP (Person with feet up on chair)	
820.	FaNS	

821.	FaiNT	
822.	FiNaNce	
823.	VeNoM	
824.	VaNaR (Monkey)	
825.	FunNeL	
826.	FiNiSH	
827.	FaNKar (Singer)	
828.	FuN Fair	
829.	Vshape NiB	
830.	ViMS	

831.	VoMiT	
832.	ForeMaN	
833.	For MoM (Asking postman as he hands you parcel)	
834.	FarMeR	
835.	FeMaLe	
836.	FaMe Shy (Someone who avoids the limelight)	
837.	FarM Key	
838.	HalF MoVe (Someone going to make a chess move and changing their mind)	
839.	FuMBle / VaMP	
840.	FiRS (Fir trees)	

841.	FluRT	
842.	FeRN	
843.	FiRM	
844.	FRaR (to run away)	
845.	FuRL	
846.	FReSH	
847.	FoRK	
848.	HooVeR ofF (Vacuum some crumbs off chair)	
849.	FiRe Place	
850.	FelLS (mountain sides)	

851.	FLaT	
852.		
853.	FLaMe	
854.	FuLeR	
855.	FaLL (water fall)	
856.	FLaG	
857.	FLocK (Group)	
858.	FLuFy	
859.	FilL uP (Car at petrol station)	
860.	FudGeS (Several fudge sweets)	

861.		
862.	FaSHioN	
863.	ViSHwaMitra	
864.	ForGeR (Making counterfeit money)	
865.	FudGe HilL (Hill made of fudge, in which your feet sink as you climb)	
866.	FiSH SHop	
867.	ViJaK (Vishakpattnam)	
868.	FetCH Pie	
869.	FiSH Pie	
870.	ViKaS	

871.	VenKaT	
872.	WaVe CaNe (Someone waving cane)	
873.	VaCuuM	
874.	FaKiR (Muslim or Hindu religious person)	
875.	FicKLe (Changeable person)	LITTLE MISS FICKLE
876.	Free KaJu	
877.	Free CaKe	
878.	Free CofFee	
879.	ForK Pea (Spearing a pea with your fork)	
880.		

881.	ViViD	
882.	FiVe New (Five new members of group)	
883.	Free FoaM	
884.	FeVeR	
885.	Free FLow (Salt)	
886.	Free FiSH	
887.	FeViCol	
888.	ViViFy (To animate)	
889.	V.ViP	
890.	Few PeaS	

891.	HalFPoT (Half a saucepan)	
892.	ViPiN	
893.	Few P.M (See a few Prime Minister)	
894.	ViPeR	
895.	ViPuL	
896.	ViPaSHa	
897.	FlopPy Kit	
898.	FliP oFf	
899.	FiBer Boards	
900.	PaSS	

901.	PaSTe	
902.	PoiSoN	
903.	BhaSM	
904.	BuZzeR	
905.	PuZzeL	
906.	PaSsaGe	
907.	BuSK (entertaining)	
908.	BSF	
909.	BiShoP	
910.	PaDS	

911.	PeTiTe (Small)	
912.	PaTterN (Knitting pattern)	
913.	BotToM	
914.	PeTeR	
915.	PeTaL	
916.	PoTaGe (Plants in greenhouse)	
917.	PaTaKa (Cracker)	
918.	PTV (Pakistan TV)	
919.	BeeDi Pee	
920.	PaNS	

921.	PaiNT	
922.	BaNaNa	
923.	PiN eM (Tailor pinning trousers for alterations)	
924.	BaNneR	
925.	PaNeL	
926.	PaNaCHe (Person with style)	
927.	PaNiK (Frightened person)	
928.	BaNVas	
929.	PiN uP (Photo)	
930.	PMS(memory techniques)	

931.	PMT exams	
932.	BowMaN	
933.	Be MuM	
934.	BiMaR (Sick)	
935.	BiMaL	
936.	Buy MuG	
937.	PuMKin	
938.	BeaM ofF (Car switching headlights off)	
939.	PiMP	
940.	PuRSe	

941.	BiRD	
942.	BuRN	
943.	BuRMa	
944.	BaRbeR	
945.	PeaRL	
946.	BRidGe	
947.	PoRK	
948.	BuRFi	
949.	PooRaB (East / Sun)	
950.	PLuS (sign)	

951.	BeLT	
952.	PLaN	
953.	PaLM	
954.	ParLoR (Beauty Parlor)	
955.	BiLL	
956.	PoLiSH	
957.	PilLocK (Stupid person)	
958.	PulL ofF (Pulling off sock)	
959.	BuLB (roots)	
960.	PaGeS	

961.	PGT Teacher	
962.	PiGeoN	
963.	PuSH Me (Asking someone to push you on a swing)	
964.	PitCHeR (Water vessel)	
965.	PaGaL	
966.	BaJaJ (Scooter)	
967.	PuSHpaK	
968.	Pea-CHeF (Chef holding lot of peas)	
969.	BJP (Bhartiya Janta Party)	
970.	BaKwaSs (movie)	

971.	PocKeT	
972.	BiKaNer (Bhujia)	
973.	PicK Me	
974.	PoKeR	
975.	PicKLe	
976.	PacKaGe	
977.	PeaCocK	
978.	BreaK Fast	
979.	PerK uP (Person suddenly looking happier)	
980.	BeVieS (more than one wife)	

981.	Bee FooT	
982.	BhaWaN (House)	
983.	Be FaMous	
984.	PVR (Cineplex)	
985.	BaFfaLo	
986.	PaV-CHai (Bread & Chai)	
987.	PufFed Cake	
988.	PuFF	
989.	BeeF uP	
990.	PiPeS	

991.	PiPeTte (Laboratory instrument for sucking up small amounts of liquid)	
992.	PoP iN (Neighbour popping in for a chat)	
993.	Bum BuM (For Shivji)	
994.	PaPeR	
995.	PiPaL (a scared tree)	
996.	PiPaGe (Lots of pipes around the room)	
997.	PoP Corns	
998.	Power PufF	
999.	PiPe uP	

Chapter 7

MNEMONIC TECHNIQUES OF ASSOCIATION

Mnemonic techniques are the basic tools for registration in our memory. It is also for improving our retention and recollection from our memory. Named after Mnemosyne, the Greek Goddess of memory, mnemonic techniques are simple methods to develop the memory power. They include unusual ways of memorising large amounts of information. A number of different techniques are used to associate something with something that we

own personal meaning system or interpretation with known images, etc. These techniques were of unbelievable importance hundreds of years ago before the invention of printing presses. Most of the people did not have access to pens and paper or printed materials that time. Relying on their own memories was the way of paramount importance. Indeed, for the ancient Greeks and Romans, mnemonic techniques are one of the most important subjects taught in classical schools. Since this is a method, we need to practice it over and over in order to become comfortable with it. Mnemonic techniques don't rely on magic but on our own ability to visualise, making connections or associations and organising important information.

First-letter Cueing:

example:

a. How many planets are there in our solar system?

You can remember the sentences: "My Very Educated Mother Just Showed Us Nine Planets", which stand for Mercury, Venus, Earth, Mars, Jupiter, Saturn, Uranus, Neptune and Pluto.

b. In mathematics we have the rule of 'BODMAS': Brackets, Off, Divide, Multiplication, Addition and Subtraction.

Acronyms:

bodies use acronyms. For example ISRO stands for Indian Space Research Organisation. Some acronyms become so familiar that we forget what the letter stands for. For example LASER,

ASH stands for Action on Smoking & Health and SEA for Shipbuilding Exports Association.

Acrostics:

series of words, lines, or verses forms the information to be remembered. For example, the trigonometry formulae for Sin, Cos, Tangent is mostly known as PANDIT BADRI PRASAD HAR HAR BOLE, SONA CHANDI TOLE. The only problem with acronym or acrostics is the tendency to forget the system we devise. To remove this possibility, try making a visual association with the shortcut. In above example we can visualise a Panditjee named Badri Prasad is praying by chanting HAR HAR and after that weighing gold and silver to donate.

Creating Own Images for Memorising or Developing Personalised Meaning System (PMS) of Data

With the help of PMS – Personalised Meaning System you will be able to memorise your syllabus. To learn this memory technique you have to visualise the words. But before that you will have to detect a meaning of the word that you hear or say. You will have to convert the words into pictures in order to give them a meaning and retain them for longer time. I will try to explain this through the following examples:

Following is the list of some minerals and their corresponding location. Suppose you have to memorise this list in one reading, then you wil have to apply the PMS method.

PMS	LIST I	LIST II
I & II	coal/steel	Jharia/Raniganj/Rourkela
III	Brass Utensils	Muradabad
IV	Cement	Katni
V	HMT Watch	Pinjor

As you have seen all the objects on the left hand side of the list, you don't have to make any PMS for them but for their location you will have to make one. I will explain it to you. See that coal is found in Jharia and Raniganj.

PMS I – coal is lying in bush (in Hindi) and it is black coal in brown   .

PMS II – see that Rani Mukherjee has gone   (bald) (Raniganj). Because her hair is being burnt with coal.

PMS III – P. V. Narsimha Rao is eating a   (banana) (Rourkela). But you can see that this banana is made of steel. It is making his teeth fall.

PMS IV – visualise that there are many people in a procession having brass utensils in their hands and shouting "murdabad, murdabad"! (Muradabad).

PMS V – your knee has got a cut (   ) and a doctor is plastering it with cement.

PMS VI – visualise that many people are making HMT watches and to do their work fast, they are saying to each other 'PINJOR' (pinjor), i.e. connect all the pins in the watch so that the output increases.

In this way you will visualise each and everything related to the product and its location. They will get imbibed deep in your mind and you will be able to recall them as when required.

Instead of mugging up the facts you can visualise them and therefore remember them automatically.

MNEMONIC STRATEGY OF LOCI SYSTEM

The oldest known mnemonic strategy (it dates to 500 B.C.) is the method of Loci. Loci are the plural of Locus, which means place or location. The loci system was used as a memory tool by both Greek and Roman orators, who took advantage of the technique to speak without notes. They would visualise objects that represented the topics they wanted to discuss, and then mentally place the objects in different locations within a building. As an orator spoke, he would mentally move through the building, retrieving the imaginary objects from each

place". The method of loci was the most popular mnemonic system until about the middle of the 1600s, when other strategies (such as the phonetic and peg systems) were introduced. This method is based on the assumption that people best remember familiar locations. Therefore, these locations can serve as clues to help in remembering information associated with them. To use the method of loci effectively, all we have to do is linking something we want to remember with a location. When we want to recall the information, we simply remember the location.

Steps of Loci System:

First, choose a place we know well, such as our house.

Secondly, visualise a series of locations in that place in a logical order. For example, begin with the front door, go through the hall, turn into the living room, proceed through the dining room and then into the kitchen. As we enter each location, always move logically and consistently in the same direction, from one side of the room around to the others. Each piece of furniture or architectural elements of the house can serve as an additional location.

Thirdly, associate each piece of information in the order it is to be remembered with a particular location in the house and visualise the association.

Remember the following items:

Paper, carrots, ice cream, rice, edible oils.

Visualise the front door is covered with the paper and now enter into the hall and see the hall is full of carrots and you are eating the tasty carrots. Now enter into the living room and see you are offered an ice cream and you taste the ice cream. Now enter into the dining room where

This method can be used for making a variety of lists, for speeches, names, and various other things to do, even to remember a thought we want to keep in our mind. The loci system works so well because it alters the way we remember. It allows us to use familiar locations to cue ourselves about things we want to recall. Because the locations are organised in a natural order, one memory easily leads into the next, dragging with it whatever information we have attached to the location.

We can enlarge the system by adding other locations we know well.

For example:
easily walk through a neighbourhood, or visualise our garden. It is also possible to add more than one item to any location.

For example: If we want to remember a list of 50 items to be purchased at the store, we could theoretically place 5 items at each of 10 locations with mnemonic strategy of association.

Memorising Speech by using Loci System

Most of the time you are being scrutinised and continuously watched during the examination period. It is done just to ensure that during the examination you are not using any unfair means. All this leads to extra pressure and it is seen that under such situations you tend to forget or your memory doesn't work properly. To get going in such trying conditions and that too in front of your teacher's eyes, you will have to use the 'Loci System' to overcome the situation. This will help you recall the answer on the spot.

This method is a boon for all those who are invited to the stage for a speech and cannot

and also ignore eye-to-eye contact with the audience in case of delivering a speech without preparations. They have to face a great deal of embarrassment at times when they forget their speech on table or when they miss some point during delivering a speech. By using Loci System your speech will be perfectly all right and while delivering it you will be able to express yourself fully through your hand movements, gestures and eye-to-eye contact with the audience. This will not only impress the organisers and audience alike but will

have a very attentive look at the venue of your speech or examination hall. You have to associate all the keywords of your speech to these objects and while you are speaking, instead of a written speech, you have to look at all the objects and surroundings. At the same time you have to give an indication, while speaking, to the various directions of objects and that's all. You will complete your speech comfortably and because of your way of delivery, you will earn accolades from one and all.

I will explain it with an example of my friend Mr Biswaroop Roy Choudhary, who is a Guiness Book of World Record holder and also as India's strongest memory man. When he goes for a seminar for memory demonstration, he comes across many objects such as fans,

windows, dining hall, utensils and parking place of cars, bikes and trees (which are outside

the seminar hall), etc., inside the seminar hall. These objects help him instantly prepare a speech.   if he has to deliver a speech on characteristics of a good leader, he asks his audience to provide him with some points about the subject, i.e. characteristics of a good leader. Some of the suggestions that he gets are:

A good leader should have the followings characterstics:

Vision	Intelligence
Responsibility	Knowledge
Health	Followers
Commanding ability	Good speaking ability
Learned person	Charismatic appearance

While linking or associating each point with these objects he would look at them very carefully

He just memorises these points, but at the same time he would link each of them with the above-mentioned objects in the following way by creating his own Personalised Meaning System or Mnemonics (PMS):

Now we will memorise this:

1. **Vision:** Vision Projector (A good projector has a good vision).
2. **Intelligent:** Intelligent student Chair (intelligent students sit on Chairs).
3. **Responsibility:** Rush with sponge Table (People are rushing to clean table with sponge).
4. **Knowledge:**   (tap) at edge Windows (
5. **Health:** See exercise Door (A person is exercising near the door).
6. **Followers:** Following Air conditioner (People are following each other and   standing near the Air Conditioner to get cool air).
7. **Commanding ability:** Come & mend Parking (A man is shouting at the parking   to come and mend the cars).
8. **Good speaking ability:**
9. **Learned personality:** Learning lessons on Sofa set (A person is sitting on a Sofa and learning lessons).
10. **Charismatic Appearance:** Karishma Kapoor-Tree (Karishma Kapoor is sitting on a tree.)

speech in the following manner:

While looking at the projector, he says that a good leader should be a good visionary. Then he looks at the chair and says he should be intelligent as well and by looking towards the table he says that a leader should be a responsible person. In this way people sitting near the table will feel addressed and taken care of.

Throughout his speech he will look towards all the objects and carry on with his speech without forgetting any point – Knowledgeable (window), healthy (Door), followers (A.C), commanding ability (Parking), (here because parking is outside the hall and as he mentions it through movement of his eyes and hands, people sitting at the last rows also would feel addressed), good speaker (Fans), learned personality (Sofa sets), charismatic (Tree). In this way he would look at different directions for recollection with the help of memory triggers, which

can link the important points of their answers during or before the start of exams to the various objects present in the examination hall. According to the feedback of almost thousands of people, this method has helped them and their performance has enhanced dramatically.

Chapter 8

SAVING DATA WITH LINK METHOD

The link method, also known as the chain system, is the most basic of the mnemonic strategies. It is used for memorising short lists of items, such as a shopping list, in which each item is linked to the next. Here is how to perform the link system:

1. Form a visual image for each item in the list.

3. Associate the image for the third item with the image for the second item and so on.

   to recall the lists.

It is important not to try to associate every item with every other item. Instead, we are just associating the two items at a time. While creating visual association, we must see vividly by our third eye. Although a funny or unusual association is good, what is most important is

remember the same association.

Some Tips on the Image Making in the Link System:

Make visual images involving all senses and you as well. We visualise through our senses of seeing, hearing, touching, tasting and smelling and also involve action or movement. One should use visualisation to check on the state of one's imaginative memory as follows:

Hearing: With eyes closed one can visualise the wind producing musical notes.

Sight:

Touch: Visualise you are holding a chilled soft drink bottle and feel the chilling sensation.

Taste: Visualise you are sitting in a restaurant and being served a sumptuous meal.

Movement: Think you are pacing up and down in a park. The grass there is wet and you are pacing briskly. But all this while you have got to keep yourself relaxed so that the imaginative skills are retained and not lost. Make solid images of abstract ideas.

Make simple and logical sequences but exaggerate the sizes and distort the features to the point of absurdity of the objects involved so that they become easy to remember.

Use humorous and colourful images

Use hyperbole: In order to reproduce a number of words from a memory in a particular sequence, experts recommend use of hyperbole (exaggeration), multiplications, substitutions, etc.

Visualise your mental pictures to be too large and out of proportion to the objects size. *For* , think of a needle, which is a metre long, surprised? But there is no harm in thinking so. After all you have not to pay for visualising things. Next, think of a fountain pen that is as large as a tree.

Substitute your items; it is simply thinking of an other item instead of the earlier one. Supposing you want to memorise two items, a birthday cake and a book.

Visualise the cake is rectangular. Try to cut it. The knife does not pass through. Examine closely. It is a book with a cover like chocolate. To sum up we can say that visualise things in action, out of proportion, illogically, colourful, in 3-dimension and use all your senses to get it impressed in the memory.

Limitation of Links

We may have already spotted one of the problems with this system – each item is linked to the

we forget one item on the linked list, the item that it is linked with next may also be forgotten. The loci method has an advantage over the link system that even if one item is forgotten, it will not affect the memory for the next item, because all of the items are linked to an unforgettable place, not to each other.

Both the link and loci methods can be used to remember items in order. However, neither of these memory techniques allows us to locate just one particular item on the list.   if

walk through our house step-by-step until we arrived at the tenth item. On the other hand, this weakness is true of most lists that we have thoroughly learned in a serial way. It is much easier to recite the letters of the alphabet in order than to name them all in a random sequence.

Aware of this, the ancients did come up with one way around it when using the loci method.

only to visualise the tenth location quickly, and then we can move ahead to the eleventh. The same strategy can be used with linking, link a $5 bill between the fourth and sixth link.

STORY SYSTEM

In older times, story telling was a favourite pass-time. Sages passed on their knowledge to their disciples who had to preserve it in their minds and later pass it on to others. A close cousin to the link system is the story system, in which each item in a list is linked to the one after it by an inter-connected story. The story system is different from the link method, in which each of the items is linked by an integrated narration. This logical sequence may be easier for people to recall the analyst of simple but un-related paired associations. On the other hand, the story

how many items are there in the link method. In link method we can recall the item either

Scientist's View about Link & Story System

Scientists who have studied the link and story system have found that both systems can help people learn and remember word lists. In fact, there is evidence that those who learn through the link system can remember up to three times as much as those who don't learn the techniques. Researches have also revealed that the story method is effective with abstract words and that un-related sentence can be remembered when they were strung together as a story. Both methods have also been shown to be more effective than the use of imagery or rehearsal alone. When the order of the recall was important, the superiority of these mnemonic techniques was even greater.

Chapter 9

Peg systems are probably the best known of all the memory systems. The use of peg words is a type of mnemonic strategy in which items to be remembered are mentally pegged to (associated with) certain images in a pre-arranged order. This method is superior to both the link and loci methods because it is not dependent on sequential retrieval. We can access any item on the list without having to work our way through all the items before it. There are a number of similarities between peg and loci methods. In both items to be remembered are associated

words in the peg method and locations in the loci method are used in the same fashion, and both peg words and locations can be used over and over again. Recall is also similar for both.

Thus the peg system is a memory technique in which standard set of peg words (concrete nouns) are learned and items to be remembered are linked to the pegs with visual imagery. The system got its name from the fact that peg words act as mental pegs or hooks on which a person hangs the information that needs to be remembered. It is the most famous mnemonic device, popular with entertainers and students of memory training. The pegs words help organise material that needs to be remembered and act as reminders to recall the material. A number of studies have shown that people are able to use the peg system effectively on lists up to 40 words long. It can also be used for remembering ideas, and similar applications.

There are a number of different peg systems, all of which use a concrete object to represent each number. The difference lies in the various ways to choose the objects that represent each number. The system includes the rhyme method, look-alike method (shape method), Phonetic peg method and the value method. Most peg systems do not include a peg word for 0. The rhyme method uses Hero for Zero and value method uses Zero as an empty box, phonetic peg uses 'Sea for zero' and look-alike method uses Zero as Bangles, etc.

Chapter 10

SAnd when the exams knock the door, they end up sticking to guidebooks. Most of us, in our

on the brain and his brother Bary Buzan, a professor at the London school of Economics, penned "The Mind Map Book," ground breaking, colourful note-making techniques which propounded the idea of "Radiant Thinking" and its best natural expression: mind mapping. Mind maps are also termed as "The Swiss army knife for the brain".The colourful mind maps, where we see more of the pictures in colours leave indelible mark on the network of tunnels (suggested by the guru of lateral thinking Edward De Bono) in your brain. And the results are incredible, because colours and pictures are one of the memory languages of the mind.

People from all walks of life, for example, Leonardoda Vinci, Isaac Newton, Albert Einstein, Thomas Edison, Beethoven, James Joyce, Vincent van Gogh, Mark twain – all used mind

standard linear note taking style of students at all levels in school, college and university, allows only part of the complete picture to us as there is no free radiation of ideas. These notes lack the visual rhythm and pattern, colour, image, visualisation, association, dimension, spatial awareness, etc., hence nothing new emerges. This technique utilises only a fraction of the brain's enormous learning potential.

Mind mapping is the concept of radiant thinking that brings the gigantic data resting in our brain cells to its logical conclusion, where we start learning in a better and fasterway.

Radiant thinking refers to the associative thought processes that proceed from or connect to a central point, leading to a coloured graphic image called mind map. It provides a universal key to unlocking the potential of the brain. The mind map harnesses the full range of cortical skills- words, image, number, logic, rhythm, colour and spatial awareness – in a single, uniquely powerful technique.

Thus mind mapping is a form of note-taking that works in harmony with the way your brain works which integrates functions of left hemispheres (words, numbers, order, sequence, and lines) and right hemispheres (colour, images, dimension, and symbols)

Example of a speech on retirement at a farewell party:

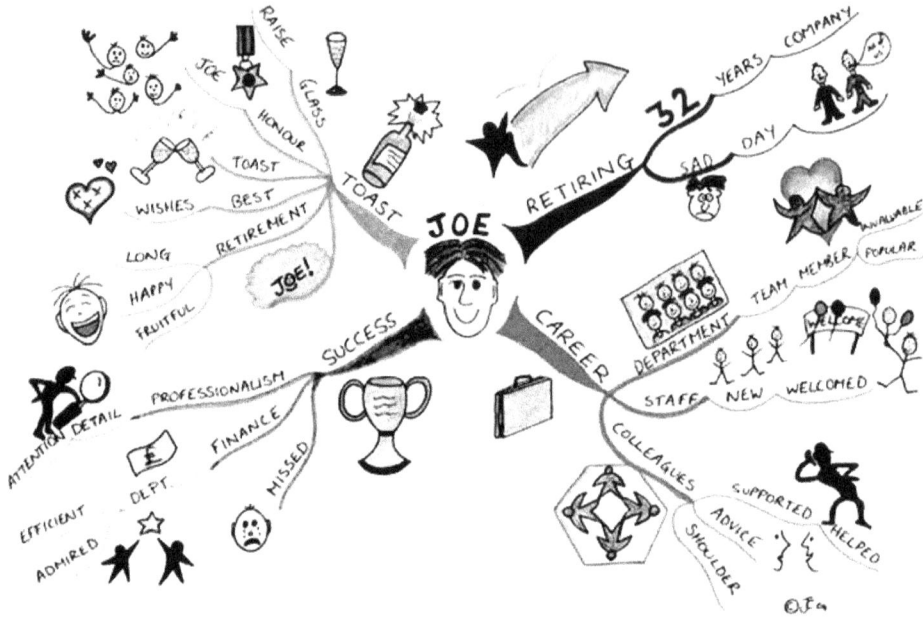

HOW TO START MIND MAPPING

In the beginning, the mind mapper creates a central theme from which associations spread in the form of branches and sub-branches and so on. Every key word or image thus added itself, brings the possibility of a new and greater range of associations. More and more related and unrelated ideas occur during the process, forming patterns of association. In order to create a

a host of other concepts can be organised. For example, the term 'machines' contains a vast array of categories, one of which is 'motor vehicles'. This in turn, generates a large range, one of which is 'cars'. This brings in the type of car such as Maruti that can again be sub-divided into various models. So machines would be BOI not Maruti as 'machines'.

If mind mappers give more emphasis to colours, pictures, codes, dimensions, diagrams, numbers, etc., their mindmaps become more interesting and entertaining which, in turn, aid creativity, enhance memory and specially the recall of information.

The full power of the mind map is realised by having a central image instead of a central word, and by using images wherever appropriate rather than words. The capacity of memorising picture is almost limitless. Pictures are evocative than words, more precise and potent intriggering a wide range of associations, there by enhancing creative thinking and memory.

Mind map laws:

Put emphasis on the following:

       Always use a central image

Comprehensive Memory Development Course

Use images throughout your mind map

Use more colours per central image

Use dimension in images and around words

Use kinaesthesia (the blending of the physical senses)

Use variations of size of printing, line and image

Use organised spacing

Use appropriate spacing

Use association

Use arrows when you make connections within and across the branch pattern

Use colours

Use codes.; be clear

Use only one key per line

Use capital letters for all words

Use capital key words on lines

Make the line length equal to word length

The three 'As' of mind mapping are:

1. **Accept:** Accept means one should set aside any preconceptions one may have about one's mental limitations and follow the mental mapping laws and recommendations correctly.
2. **Apply:** It is the second stage for developing our own mind mapping style.
3. **Adapt:** It refers to the ongoing development of the mind mapping skills.

Thus, after following the mind mapping laws, one can reach a stage where things become immensely clear. With the help of well-crafted mind map, we can organise ours as well as other people's ideas; enhance memory; think creatively; create a group mind by bringing individuals together; analyse yourself; solve personal problems; maintain a mind map diary; presentations; management; teaching; story-telling, etc. Choice is enormous.

Memory Technique of Mental Filing System

the storehouse of our memory bank and facilitate easy recall to the showroom of our conscious mind whenever we need them. Effective usage of this system enables us to store any amount of

The human brain has no match in sorting out, storing and recalling information. It can beat

device. But still we do not rely on our natural memory system and retain diaries, index books, notebooks, digital diaries and other memory aids.

depending on the nature of work, but the most common criterion is subject. Files on similar subject

may be indexed. Old sites may be recorded and stored in a separate place, which may be away from the immediate work place.

closed and stored.

In many respects, the mind works like a computer. It is, therefore, very necessary that after giving the mind an order to note something properly and memorise it, we must help the mind

the name of familiar person immediately on meeting him or her. We must keep on talking and recalling what we have to say next in a speaking assignment. So there is simply no scope to

fact must exist as distinctly as possible. Our brain is just like the hard disk of a computer. As we

will. The key is to store the information in a systematic manner.

Creation of Mental Files:

For examples:

relatives, friends, teachers, role models, sports person, actor, actress, god and goddesses, etc.

to recall the digits by using their association later.

For example:

Sl. No.	
1.	Mother's name
2.	Father's name
3.	Aunt's name
4.	Uncle's name
5.	Sister's name
6.	Brother's name
7.	Sister-in-law's name

8.	Brother-in-law's name
9.	Goddess Laxmi
10.	God Narayana & so on.

Suppose you want to memorise the properties of an electron. Give name to the electron as No

extra tools apart from other mental pegs to memorise anything.

Mental Filing Works Better with Comprehension Method

It is the method of remembering by understanding. This procedure works well for science subjects, where understanding of the procedure or the process becomes very important. Try to comprehend the subject under six headings –   and   . Hence after reading the matter once, try to understand what you have read by asking these questions. It is a permanent way of remembering.

Regarding your studies ask the following questions to yourself:

What are my problems regarding studies?

When should I start preparing for my examinations?

Why am I tensed about studies and examinations?

How can I overcome my tension and stress regarding studies?

Where should I start studying from?

Whose help should I take or whom should I consult regarding my studies?

Change your study method

of ten minutes. The question is what you need to do during this ten minute break?

As we know, "comprehending and recalling" are very important parts of memory, so we need to practice the same. After reading for an hour, sit in another chair, close your eyes and try to recall what you have read for the last one hour. Initially, you will be shocked to see that you can hardly recall anything. After 10 minutes of this exercise, go back for reading once again.

and recalling ability. Hence, there will be no question of you missing any information in the examination hall.

Use of mechanical method where comprehension method does not work

The mechanical method of remembering is also called the 'by heart' method or rote method of

names, multiplication tables, etc. This method should not be used for remembering procedures or processes. Comprehension method is very useful to memorise procedures and processes.

Many students and adults use this method in their day-to-day life. As repetition is the mother

continuous repetition, can very easily recite many rhymes. The child does not even know the meaning of "twinkle, twinkle, little star, how I wonder what you are….." But he or she can still recite the poem. Similarly, priests in temples or in churches can narrate number of '   ' or verses because they have been doing it repeatedly. Even students can do the same. The only problem is that with many subjects and many chapters to be memorised in a short span of time, students have a lot on their plate. To make this method work, after every hour of study, students need to recall and recap what they have learnt to see how much they can actually reproduce in an examination. If anything is missing it needs to be strengthened by a second reading. This method is much better than trying to cram huge masses of information at one go without checking how much of it has really sunk in.

paste it on a wall above your study or worktable. Read, observe and revise these for 10 minutes twice a day – preferably in the morning and at night. The results are almost instantaneous.

will never need to look at the chart again.

Hence, it is very important to know how we can do about the repetition process in a productive manner. The right procedure is to read today and repeat the same thing tomorrow. For example, spend four hours today to read chapter-I, tomorrow, when you repeat, you will require only 15 minutes to revise Chapter-I, the rest of the time can be spent on reading chapter-II. On third

time on chapter III. As you keep going, once in a fortnight, revise all the chapters. If you keep repeating this, all the chapters will be fresh in your mind on any given day.

To remember formulae, wherever you think you may go wrong, write these formulae in different colour. They stay in our subconscious mind for a long time. Red colour is more preferable as it has the longest wavelength and so it stands out more in comparison to the other colours.

PART : II

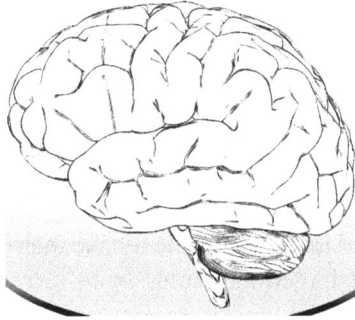

Applications of Memory Techniques

Chapter 1

The most common complaint made by people who consider themselves to possess poor memory, is that they are continually forgetting people's names. They remember the faces (images are easy to recall), but the names fail to stick. The problem of forgetting names can be a big one, particularly if you work in an environment which involves meeting a large number of new clients, who may take offence if you are continually getting their names wrong.

In fact they may even be so insulted that they decide to take their business elsewhere. A terrible calamity indeed! The problem of forgetting names is an extremely common one, which is experienced by most people throughout their lives. But fortunately it is a problem that can be

In this section we will discuss two basic methods, which when used in conjunction with one another, will enable you to remember a large number of individuals' names associated with their respective faces, after hearing them only once. This is an incredibly useful skill to possess and is particularly useful on such occasions as parties, business meetings and various other kinds of work-related or social gatherings. The methods are:

1. Observational system
2. Association system

But before outlining these systems I would just like to bring to your attention a particularly pertinent fact. That is that faces are not processed by the human brain in the same way that other information is. In 1971, scientists Goldstein and Chance conducted a series of tests in

and inkblots. Fourteen from each were shown for three seconds at a time and following an interval of 48 hours the subjects recall was tested.

It was then found that faces were the most easily recalled, this was followed by inkblots, and

part of human perception.

The Observational system

in memory, is to somehow give their name meaning, so that it may be easily visualised.

For example: the name 'Jhonson' can easily be broken down into two words – Jhon & Son. These words possess meaning, and anything that contains meaning is far more memorable than something that does not.

The name 'Greensmith' could be separated into the two words Green and Smith. The colour green is obviously fairly easy to visualise. Also smith (to me anyway) immediately conjures up the image of a 'blacksmith'.

Dish. Again these two words are simple to visualise.

Some of the names that you will come across are obviously far easier than others to visualise. For example, the names Green, White, Brown and Black (being colours), already possess meaning and thus require no further processing in order to visualise them. Same with the names Peacock, York, Smiley and Forester.

Other names may, however, require a little more effort to transform into a meaningful phrase,

any name – no matter how abstract – into an easily visualisable form. However, to help you on your way, I have listed, at the end of this section, a large variety of different names, together with appropriate mental imagery.

The purpose of splitting an abstract name into a non-abstract collection of words is to allow your brain to categorise the information that is contained within the name; something that the human

Also the act of transposing a name into a meaningful form, forces an individual to observe that name, and as was explained in an earlier section, observation is the most important prerequisite of an individual's memory.

The Associational System

After breaking down a name that you wish to recall into an easily visualisable image (or set of images), the next step is to link that image to the individual concerned.

To accomplish this, you simply need to pick out the features or characteristics of the individual that stand out the most to you. This could be a dimple on his chin, or a freckle on her nose, or even a limp in their left leg.

Other things that you could use are – big ears, a hooked nose, wide forehead, a large or a small mouth, full or thin lips, or even a pair of bushy eyebrows. You could also choose something less visual, such as a lisp, or a stutter as the feature of the person that stands out the most to you.

Whatever the feature that you choose is, linking it to a name should not present you with much of a problem. If you are familiar with the link method, I have listed a few examples below to show you exactly what I mean.

Examples:

1. In order to remember a woman whom you have just been introduced to – who happens to have long, red hair – goes by the name of Miss Fields. All that you would need to do,

   red hair spread out around her head.
   See it twisting around the long green grass. You might also try exaggerating the length of

   you see her (and her hair) again, you will immediately be reminded of her name '**Fields**.'

2. To remember a man named Mr. Taylor who you

   outstanding feature (say thick eyebrows) and imagine him with eyebrows so long that they reach down to the

   Imagine him in this amusing predicament, whilst he is in the process of being measured for a new suit by his tailor. Thus powerfully linking his most outstanding feature to his name.

   Ex. 2

3. In order to remember the name Mr Adamson who is of a tall, thin man, that you have just been introduced to, you

   '**Adamson**.'

4. To remember the name of a dimpled young lady named Miss Standwick, you could try picturing her face, with a number of large candle wicks standing in her exaggeratedly oversised dimples. Stand wicks – 'Standwick.'
   If you really try hard to visualise the above image, then you

   Ex. 4

   Standwick's name.

5. Finally, to remember Mr Hill (who happens to possess a wide forehead), you could imagine a man's forehead, with a miniature mountain stuck in its centre. You might even like to visualise a large, snowy peak on its top. This is in order to make an image that much more amusing and thus more easy to recollect.

   Ex. 5

Comprehensive Memory Development Course

Chapter 2

Land locations or routes of new places. For example, let us talk about your friends. A friend of yours tells you that he has recently shifted his residence. He explains the route to you and says:

station, turn left from there. There is a pipal tree behind the third house in the adjoining street. Turn right from there. Now come straight. You will see a Pan shop. My house is towards the back of the seveneth house from this Pan shop. The house is on the main road. My house no. is 341."

Whenever we go to some new place and search the way, while someone is explaining to you, you do not even want to pay attention because you know that even after you have heard the

six places. In the visualisation or association method, words like left, right, U-turn do not get any memory picture. If in our mind we create a picture of these three we will be able to solve this problem to a great extent.

Word	PMS (visualisation)
Right	red
Left	leaf
U-turn	umbrella

If you remember 'red', 'leaf' and 'umbrella' as left, right and U-turn respectively, understanding the route will become easy because you don't need to be told when you have to go straight.

Now connect the route, places and location to these symbols:

You go a little ahead there will be a police station, turn left fron there

There is a pipal tree behind the third house in the adjoining street. Turn right from there.

Now come straight. You will see a pan shop. My house is towards the back of the seveneth house from this Pan shop.

The house is on the main road. My house no. is 341."

REMEMBERING NUMBERS, DATES AND FACTS

1. **1955:** Bandung Conference
   We will use PMS and phonetic codes for visualisation:

digits. We will use tri-colours of our		for 18, 19, 10. Then we will associate them.
19	white (colour)	
55	laloo	
Bandung	band (bundle) of dung (cowdung)	

Visualisation: Visualise that Lalu Yadav is in white dress and his white dress becomes dirty while he is passing through the band of dungs.

2. **1885:**

18	saffron (colour)
Karl Banz	curly bench
Germany	germs

Visualisation: A saffron colour car covered with the germs is being demonstrated for the

3. **1876:** Graham Bell discovered telephone

18	saffron (colour)
76	kaju
Graham Bell	hot bull

Visualisation: You are feeding saffron and kaju through a telephone to a hot (   ) bull to bring down its temperature.

4. **1889:** Pandit Jawahar Lal Nehru born

| 18 | saffron (colour) |
| 89 | FP (fountain Pen) |

Visualisation: Pandit Jawahar Lal Nehru chacha is writing a story with his fountain pen and also eating saffron simultaneously.

5. **1914:**

| 19 | white (colour) |
| 14 | dara singh |

The tramp trump card

Visualisation:

REMEBERING PHONE NUMBERS

to memorise. But visualisation and memory techniques are also helpful to meorise the phone numbers also.

Suppose you have to memorise the number of Annamalai University. The number is 9486874195.

So we will have to convert these digits into pictures with the help of phonetic codes and further we will associate with the institution.

Words/ digit	PMS
Annamalai	Anna Hazare is eating
94	berry
86	
87	fog
41	rat
95	bell

Now we will visualise and make a story:

Anna hazare is eating   , but suddenly somebody came with some berry and gifted to him,

aquarium and when fog suddenly vanished he found a rat is ringing a bell in the aquarium.

In this way we can memorise lot of phone numbers of persons or important individuals.

Chapter 3

MEMORISING HISTORY

Memorising historical facts

1. Mohenjodaro is situated in Sind Province in Pakistan

   PMS –

   Mohenjodaro – mohan is showing   (magic)

   Sind – Sindhi people

   Pakistan – Musharaff (President)

   Visualisation: Mohan is showing a   to Musharaff (President of Pakistan)

2. Bana Bhatta lived in the court of Harshvardahan

   PMS –

   Bana Bhatta – Mahesh Bhatt with a   (arrow) (a posture in a movie)

   Harshvardhana – Harshvardhan (laughing man)

   Visualisation: Mahesh Bhatt is htting a   (arrow) at **Harshvardhan** (laughing man).

3. The Triratnas were sessed by Mahavir

   PMS –

   Triratnas – 3   (gems)

   Visualisation: Mahavir is wearing 3 ratna.

4. The largest stupa at sanchi is assignable to the period of the Mauryas

   PMS –

   Sanchi (sun-chai) –   (tea) on sun

   Mauryas –   (peacock)

   Visualisation: is drinking   on the sun.

5. Harappan seals were made of terracotta

   PMS –

Harappan –Virrapan

Terracotta – tarcol

Visualisation: Virappan made a seal of **coal**.

6. An image of dancing girl is found at Mohanjodaro

    PMS –

    Mohajodaro – Mohan is showing   (magic)

    Visualisation: Mohan was showing   and suddenly an image of **a dancing girl** appeared

7. Buddhist literature was written in Pali

    PMS –

    Buddhist – Budh literature

    Pali –

    Visualisation: One Budha was writing a literature

8. Manu Smriti deals with law

    PMS –

    Manu – Manu (a boy)

    Smriti – Smriti Irani (Tv actress)

    Law – law books

    Visualisation: Manu and **Smriti Irani** are studying **law** books.

9. Chandragupta Maurya defeated Seleucus

    PMS –

    Chandragupta –   (gupta on moon)

    Maurya –   (peacock)

    Saleucus – salad (   )

    Visualisation: **salad**

10. The dead body of Babur was buried following his own wishes in Kabul

    PMS –

    Babur – Baabbar Bhor

    Kabul – cable

    Visualisation: Babbar Bhor was buried under **cable**.

11. The Bhakti Movement of the 16th century had as one of its leaders – Guru Nanak

    PMS –

    16 – hockey stick

    Visualisation: Visualise yourself holding a hockey stick and praying to Guru Nanak as a leader.

12. Which of the following is not true about Amir Khusro? He was a - Musician

    PMS –

    Amir Khusro – amir khan – khus

    Musician – music

Visualisation: Amir Khan is not   (happy) because of the music played by him.

13. Whose work is Bijak? – Kabir

    PMS –

    Kabir – Kabir Bedi

    Bejak – *beej* (seed)

    Visualisation: Kabir wrote a poem on *beej*

14. Krishna Dev Raya was a contemporary of Babur

    PMS –

    Krishna Dev Raya – Lord Krishna

    Contemporary –   (thorns) with   (angel)

    Babur – Babbar Bhor

    Visualisation: Lord Krishna was walking on   (thorns) with   (angel), Suddenly Baabbar Bhor arrived.

15. The Indian civil service was introduced during the rule of Cornwallis

    PMS –

    Cornwallis – corn

    Indian civil services –

    Visualisation: You are eating corn sitting on a wall and watching the movie **Ishq**.

TO MEMORISE THE NAWABS OF BENGAL

First we will create the PMS of the names of the Nawabs and then using the PMS method we will make the links. See the list of the Nawabs of Bengal.

1. Murshid-quli-khan
2. Shuja-ud-din
3. Sarfraj khan
4. Alivardi khan
5. Siraj-ud-dullah
6. Mir-jafar
7. Mir-quasim

To learn this list of Nawab you have to take the help of PMS

linking the code with the PMS of the Nawab's name which is done as follow:

Nawabs	PMS
Murshid-quli-khan	mor - coolie - khana
Shuja-ud-din	sage - den
Sarfraz khan	sir - fur - khana
Alivardi khan	aaloo - vardi (dress)
Siraj - ud - dulah	sea - raja
Mir - Jafar	meera - safar (journey)
Mir - quasim	Meera - cash

Comprehensive Memory Development Course

Visualisation:

1. **Sun:** make a mental picture that on the sun a coolie is giving   (food) to a mor.
2. **Shoe:** make a mental picture that a sage talking to a shoe in a den.
3. **Tree:** make a mental picture that on a tree, your sir is eating   and there is fur in the khana.
4. **Door:** make a mental picture that on the door you hang your   (dress) full of
5. **Knife:** make a mental picture that you are cutting the sea with the knife.
6. **Vicks:** make a mental picture that a girl called Meera applies vicks on her face and goes on a   (journey).
7. **Heaven:** make a mental picture that in heaven Meera is counting cash.

MEMORISING ANCIENT CIVILISATION

See how:

Civilisation	location
Roman	River Tiber
Sumerian	Tigris
PMS –	
Roman – Raman (a boy)	
Tiber – tub	
Visualisation: make a mental picture that your friend **Raman** is carrying a **tub**.	
Civilisation	**Location**
Sumerian	Sumo – Rain
Tigris	Tiger
Visualisation: make a mental picture that a **tiger** is driving a **Sumo** in **rain**.	

TO MEMORISING TREATISE & SOURCES OF THE HISTORY OF THE MUGHAL ERA

Name of treatise	Author
Aine-Akbari	Abul Fazl
	Mulla Daud

PMS	
Aine-Akbari	Aina (mirror) Akhbar (newspaper)
Abul-fazal	A bull – Fasal (crop)
Mulla Daud	Mulla Daud (run)

Visualisation: 1. make a mental picture that you are are reading an   (newspaper) and   (mirror). In the mirror, there is a Bull who is eating   (crop). 2. make a mental picture that a **mulla** is **running** holding a calendar and shouting that

LONG THEORY OF HISTORY

APPLICATION OF LOCI SYSTEM

Suppose we have to memorise long points or long answers. For Example:

Question: Brahmsamaj was established by Raja Ram Mohan Roy. Describe the Social reforms carried out by him?

Answer: There are six points in the answer:

1. Brahmsamaj propagates the belief in one omnipotent God.

   and superstitions.
3. Brahmsamaj condemned the Caste system.
4. Brahmsamaj condemned the rituals propagated by temple priests.
5. Brahmsamaj has 124 centres all over India.
6. Brahmsamaj condemned idol worship.

Now, we will learn these points through journey method. For using this technique, you have to know your way back home from school.

For example:

1. School gate
2. Gate of the school
3. Bus stand
4. Bus
5. Red light
6. Market
7. Temple
8. Apolo hospital
9. Flyover
10. Rose garden

13. Friend's house
14. Restaurant

17. My house

In this manner, all the landmarks dotting the way from school to house will be clearly etched in your memory. You can take help of these stops or landmarks of this journey to memorise long

Now we will learn the 6 points of Brahmsamaj with the help of above mentioned landmarks:

1. Brahmsamaj propagates the belief in one omnipotent God.

   school.

   Memory Picture: In **school**, we are taught to pray to one God.

   superstitions.

   Your next landmark is **Gate**

   Memory picture: Imagine that outside the **school gate**, child marriages and sati system are taking place, and Raja Ram Mohan Roy is protesting against them.

3. Brahmsamaj condemned the Caste system.

   Third landmark: **Bus stand**

   Memory picture: The **bus stand** is also divided on the basis of caste. People have queued up separately according to their castes. Raja Ram Mohan Roy comes there and counsels the people to be unite.

4. Brahmsamaj condemned the rituals propagated by temple priests.

   Your next landmarks – **Bus**

   Memory picture: Imagine that many priests after boarding the bus, have started doing rituals and Raja Ram Mohan Roy is telling them not to do so in the bus. He is telling that do it in your houses not in the bus.

5. Brahmsamaj has 124 centres all over India.

   Next landmark – **Red light**

   Memory picture: Apply the phonetic method and convert 124 into **DNR**. This gives us a familiar word **dinner**. Now, you can easily create a memory picture. Imagine that everyone is having **dinner** at the **red light**

6. Brahmsamaj condemned idol worship

   Your next landmark – **Market**

   Memory picture: Imagine that people are indulging in idol worship in the market. Raja Ram Mohan Roy comes there and tells them that God is one and he lives in us. So idol worship is wrong.

See how the main points of an answer can be connected to different landmarks of your journey. You can make landmarks of any places or town that you know well. For example: home landmarks, market landmarks, friend's house landmark, temple ladmarks, etc. By using them, you can easily remember or visualise long points or long theories of various questions.

Question: Write a short note on Simon Commission.

Answer: There was a virtual lull in the country's politics after the death of CR Das. However, the appointment of the Indian statutory commission in November 1927 under the chairmanship of Johan Simon broke this lull. Its main objective was to examine the working of the Government of India Act 1919 and suggest further measures to improve the Indian administration. All the members of this commission were Englishmen. This all white commission is also known as the Simon Commission.

the British Government was not interested in genuine constitutional reforms. They demanded that the Indian members in the British house of commons like S.P. Sinha must be associated with the Commission. Their argument was that only the Indians knew the nature of their problem. But the British Government rejected the demand of Indians. Instead, the Secretely of state for India Lord Birkenhead, insulted stating that the Indians were not competent to discuss constitutional issues for working out a constitutional framework acceptable to all sections of the society.

Word	PMS
John Simon	John (Abraham) is playing (a horn)
C.R. Das	Car Das
Statutory	Statue
Commission	Commission
November	Diwali (Generally Diwali falls in November)
1927	White neck
1919	White lolypops
All white	Church nuns
British govt	See Britishers
S.P. Sinha	SP (Shatrughan) Sinha
Secretary	See a secretary
Lord Birkenhead	Brick on his head

Visualisation:

1. There was a virtual lull in the country's politics after the death of CR das.

   (Visualise that there was an **empty period** (meaning of lull) in Indian politics after the death of **Das** in a **car** accident)

2. However, the appointment of the Indian statutory commission in November 1927 under the chairmanship of Johan Simon broke this lull.

   (Visualise that after the death of **Das** in India, **John Abraham** made a **statue** after taking some **commission** under his chairmanship at the time of **diwali**.)

3. Its main objective was to examine the working of the Government of India Act 1919 and suggest further measures to improve the Indian administration.

   [Visualise that **John Abraham's** main objective is to see that Govt is giving lollypops (Indian Government Act 1919) to Indian Adminisrtative service (IAS)].

4. All the members of this commission were Englishmen. This all white commission is also known as the Simon Commission.

(Visualise that **John Abraham** makes his group for making **statue** and in the group, he includes only nuns who all are dressed in white)

doubt that the British Government was not interested in genuine constitutional reforms.

(Visualise that the **Indians** didn't like this type of constitution (only included **nuns**))

6. They demanded that the Indian members in the British House of Commons like S.P. Sinha must be associated with the commission.

(Visualise that Indians are demanding that actors like **SP (Shatrughan Sinha)** should be included in the commission, who is also a member of British House of Common.

7. Their argument was that only the Indians knew the nature of their problem. But the British Government rejected the Indians' demand.

(Visualise that John and Britishers didn't like the Indians' demand).

8. Instead, the Secretely of state for India Lord Birkenhead insulted the Indians saying that Indians were not competent to discuss constitutional issues of work out constitutional framework acceptable to all sections of the society.

(Visualise that their secretary's got his head; injured by bricks because he insulted the Indians by saying that they cannot compete the Britishers in constitutional works.)

Memorising answers related to historical dates

1. DATE-647 AD

EVENT – Death of Harsha

MEMORY CODE – JeRK

PMS – Your friend **Harsha** or see an ever-laughing person or laughing Budha.

Visualisation: Harsha died when you gave him a **jerk**. Or a laughing person died of **jerk**.

2. DATE - 1469

EVENT – Birth of Guru Nanak

MEMORY CODE – Chair – Chips

PMS – Guru Nanak's photo

Visualisation: You are sitting in a big **chair** on the road and distributing **chips** packets to the people, on the eve of **Guru Nanak's** Birthday.

3. DATE - 1576

EVENT – Battle of Haldi Ghati

MEMORY CODE – Hook – Cash

PMS – Haldi

Visualisation: Battle in a ground full of Haldi, with Hook for lot of Cash.

4. DATE - 1605

    EVENT - Death of Akbar

    MEMORY CODE – Hockey – Hall

    PMS – AKHBAR (Newspaper)

    Visualisation: Visualise that you are playing **Hockey** in a **Hall** wrapped in a (Newspaper).

5. DATE - 1668

    EVENT - First French factory at Surat

    MEMORY CODE – Hockey – Chef

    PMS – French Fries

    Visualisation: A **Chef** is making **French fries** with a **Hockey** stick in a **factory**.

6. DATE - 1905

    EVENT – Partition of Bengal

    MEMORY CODE – Loly Pop – Hall

    PMS – Bengali Babu

    Visualisation: You are eating a big **Loly Pop** in a vacant **Hall** with a Bengali Babu.

7. DATE - 1921

    EVENT – Election held in Italy, no party won a Majority

    MEMORY CODE – Loly Pop – Net

    PMS – Idli

    Visualisation: Visualise a scene of election campaign, the sign is **Idli** (Italy) in shape of **Loly Pop**. You are serving this **Loly Pop** to people and covering those people with a **Net so** that they don't run away.

8. DATE- 1921

    EVENT – 2 million unemployed persons in the UK

    MEMORY CODE – Loly Pop – Net

    PMS – Britania Biscuit

    Visualisation: Visualise an unemployed person outside the factory demanding for two **Britania Biscuit**, but you are offering them **Loly Pop** and covering them with **Net**.

9. DATE - June 1941

    EVENT – Germany attached with the Soviet Union

    MEMORY CODE - 41- Rat

    PMS – Germany – many Germs. Soviet – So Rahe Hai, June – zoo

    Visualisation: Visualise a **Rat** in **Zoo**, eating those **germs** which are sleeping.

10. DATE- 1764

    EVENT – Battle of Buxar

    MEMORY CODE – Deck– Jar

PMS – Boxer

Visualisation: Make a mental picture that a **Boxer**   **Jar** on
his hands which has been kept on Deckl instead of gloves.

Important Rulers & their future

After that make a proper link. See how:

1. Babur – 1526-1530

   PMS – Babur – Dabur (chyawanprash)

   1526 – Tail – Nag

   1530 – Mess (leave 15 this time)

Visualisation: Visualise that you are applying **Dabur Chyawanprash** on the **tail** of a **Nag**; and now the **Nag** runs towards a **mess**.

2. Sher – Shah – Suri (1540 -1545)

   PMS – Sher – Shah – Suri (Sher – sari)

   1540-45 (tail – rose – rail)

Visualisation: Visualise that a **sher** is rolling a **sari** around its **tail**, now on the **tail** he is tying a rose and now, he runs towards a **rail**.

3. Bahadur Shah (1707 – 1712)

   PMS – Bahadur Shah – Bahadur (see a Nepali boy)

   1707 – Deck – heaven

   12 – Den

Visualisation: Visualise that a Nepali boy called **Bahadur** is playing his **Deck** in heaven inside a **Den**.

4. Aurangzeb – (1659 - 1707)

   PMS – Aurangzeb – orange zeb me (in pocket)

   1659 – Taj – lab

   1707 – Deck – heaven

Visualisation: Visualise that you are putting an **orange** in your **zeb** then go into the **Taj**. You
                                                        deck; you pick up the decs and take
them to **heaven**.

MEMORISING SOCIAL STUDIES

To memorise the rights of consumers under the comsumer protection Act 1986.

a) Right to Safety

b) Right to Environment

c) Right to Consumer Education

d) Right to seek Redressal

e) Right to Information

f) Right to Choose

g) Right to be Heard

PMS:

"**SEE** HOW **RICH** THE CONSUMER IS"

S	E	E

Safety	Education	Environment

R	I	C	H

Redressal	Information	Choice	Heard

TO MEMORISE FUNDAMENTAL RIGHTS

First of all we will create PMSs of the keywords of the fundamental rights and then we will make a suitable link using the second Roller.

1. Right to equality
2. Right to freedom
3. Right against exploitation
4. Right to religion
5. Right to education
6. Right to constitutional remedies

To learn these fundamental rights you have to use PMS method, link each 'Right' with the 'Code".

Keywords		PMS
Equality	-	Quality ice cream
Freedom	-	A freedom bike
Exploitation	-	Station
Religion	-	Rally-Zen
Education	-	School
Remedies	-	Ready-made

1. **Sun:** make a mental picture that you are eating **quality ice cream** sitting on the **sun**.
2. **Shoe:** make a mental picture that there is a **yellow colour freedom bike** running on your **shoe**.
3. **Tree:** make a mental picture that on a big **tree** is beign cut for constructing a railway station.
4. **Door:** make a mental picture that on a **big rally** is breaking a **Zen** car by putting stones on it.
5. **Knife:** make a mental picture that in a **school** there are a lot of **knives**.
6. **Vicks:** make a mental picture that you are applying **vicks** on the **readymade** garments to protect them.

TO MEMORISE CONSTITUTIONAL AMENDMENTS

we will establish suitable links.

Examples:

1. The twenty-second (1969) amendment – Meghalaya was created

   PMS –

Twenty-second	22 – nan
69	Chip (in phonetic)
Meghalaya	Megh (cloud)

Visualisation: Visualise that you are eating **nan** with **chips** sitting on the megh.

from 525 to 545.

PMS –

73	comb
525	lawn – knife
545	liril (soap)

Visualisation: Visualise that you are sitting on a **mat** and holding a **comb** in your hand. Now you are going towards the **lawn** holding a **knife**, and you are cuting a liril soap with that knife.

Write a short note on composition of the Supreme Court.

While memorising a long theory we have to follow the following rules:

1. First of all, we should read every line and understand the text properly.

This way, we would be able to remember all the PMS which would help us recollecting the keywords and those keywords would help us recollecting the whole text.

Answer: In India, Supreme Court is apex body of Judicial System. It consists of the Chief Justice

Appointments of the Supreme Court Judges

The Chief Justice and other judges of the Supreme Court are appointed by the President. But he is not a free hand in this matter. He must consult the Chief Justice of the Supreme Court before appointing any judge. Similarily, while appointing the Chief Justice, he consults the

Removal of the Supreme Court Judges

The Chief Justice and other judges of the Supreme Court are appointed by the President but their services cannot be terminated by him. They can resign from their posts at their own accord whenever they like. Death of course can be another cause of the end of their service before the age of retirement.

But if the judge of the Supreme Court is found guilty of misusing his power or of acting against

of impeachment of a judge is same as the president of India.

The Chief Justice of India formerly used to get Rs 10000 as a pay per month while other judges of the Supreme Court received Rs 90000 per month. But as a result of the recommendations of

the Supreme Court from Rs 9000 to Rs 30000.

They get certain special allowances as well. Their personal safety is the responsibility of the state.

PMS:

Keywords	PMS
Supreme Court	supreme chair in court
Chief justice	yourself

Judges	see a judge
25	nail
President	Abdul Kalam
Terminate	kicking
Impeached	peach (fruit)
10000	hen, 000 (hen giving three eggs together)
9000	wine + three eggs
1997	bike
30000	mess 000

Visualisation: Visualise as if you are sitting on a **supreme chair** (**you** are a chief justice) and see other judge are siting on small chair to distinguish yourself from others, you have a **nail**

Appointment / Removal of Supreme Court judges: Now visualise that you (sitting on the supreme chair) and other judges (carrying their chair with them) have been appointed for a court by **President APJ Abdul Kalam** and he cannot **kick** you out once you enter into the court. You can resign on your own, or death can be the cause of the end of your appointments.

But if you are found that you are breaking the rules of the Supreme Court, then you will be given a **peach (fruit)** and relieved from the court.

You get pay in the form of a **hen with 3 eggs (10,000)** while other judges get in the form of **wine with 3 eggs (9000)**. And if you ask for the pay sitting on a **bike (1997)** with a **knife** (5th pay commission) then you may get **(9000 to 30000) wine + 3 egg** or even **full** army **mess + 3 eggs**. Besides, **free furnished house + car + driver**.

To memorise the shortnote on 'Rural Community Development'

The objectives of the Rural Community Development are:

i. Farmers are provided with high-yielding seeds, modern agricultural implements, fertilizers and healthy cattle.

ii. Irrigation facilities are improved by construction of canals, digging wells and installing pumps.

iii. Wastelands are made suitable for agriculture by using fertilizers. Tree plantation has also been launched to stop soil erosion.

iv. Cultivators are encouraged to grow and increase the output of vegetables and fruits.

v. Modern methods of farming are taught.

vi. Schools and adult education centres are opened.

vii. Health care centres and family welfare centres are set up.

For memorising these points, you have to **see yourself as a person, wearing rural clothes and standing on the roof of a hut.** Now see that on a normal rural day, people are going for their jobs and women and children are enjoying a sunny day.

see yourself talking to a farmer, asking about seeds, its quality and price.

See that

The basic thrust of this sort of visualisation is to enliven the very content in full spirit so that everything gets solidly stored in the mind. Suppose you want to remember a list of abstract ideas; say you need to give a speech or presentation. **Translate the abstract ideas into visual images of tangible objects.**
graph. If you need to mention product distribution, picture a truck or a train. If you need to talk about a change in management attitude, envision a manager upside down. When you need to recall series of ideas, just recall the objects.

To memorise the powers of President: The President of India is the highest executive authority. The constitution vests in him all the executive powers of the union. All executive actions are taken in his name. He is the head of the State and represents the Republic of India.

Power or Functions: The President performs a number of functions. He has vast powers to be exercised during normal times as well as in emergencies. These powers, however, are actually exercised by the Prime Minister and the Council of Ministers.

I. Executive Powers

The constitution vests in the President of India and all the central government. He appoints the Prime Minister, who enjoys the support of the majority in the Lok Sabha. He also appoints other members of the council of ministers and distributes portfolios to them on the advice

Lok Sabha. As long as the majority in the Lok Sabha supports the government, the council of ministers cannot be dismissed. The President is the supreme commander of the Defence Forces of India. He can declare war, make peace and conclude treaties with other countries.

The President makes important appointments. He appoints the Governors of States, Chief Justice, Judges of the Supreme Court and the High Courts, Attorney General, Comptroller and Auditor General, Chief Election Commissioner, and other Auditor Commissioners, Chairman and Members of the Union Public Service Commission and Ambassadors, High Commissioners to other countries. He also receives the credentials of Ambassadors and High Commissioners from other countries.

WORD	PMS
Prime Minister	Manmohan Singh
Governors of State	GAON (Village)
Chief Justice	Yourself (Sitting on a big chair) judge of Supreme Court
High Court	Judge sitting on a supreme chair on a height
Attorney general	Atta general
Comptroller	Computer on roles
Auditor general	Auditorium
Chief election commissioner	Chef contesting for election, asking for commission
Other election commissioner	Other people contesting election
Chairman	chair
Member of UPSC	Oops movie
Ambassadors	car (ambassador)
High commission	high commission (taking lots of money as commission)

Visualisation: APJ Abdul Kalam is giving an axe to Manmohan Jee and asking him to go to a GAON (Village), **where a chief is contesting for election & is asking for High Commission;**

Chief. Then he sees that a Judge is sitting on a Supreme Chair on a height, Manmohan Jee asks for **Atta** to prepare roti. He puts   in the computer and goes to an Auditorium, sits there on a Chair and watch Oops movies. Suddenly his Car (Ambassadors) comes and he moves back to APJ Abdul kalam.

II. Judicial Powers

As the supreme executive head, the President can grant pardon or reduce the sentence of any convicted person. If he considers that a question of law or a matter of public importance has arisen, he can ask for the advisory opinion of the Supreme Court. He may or may not accept that opinion.

WORD	PMS
Judicial Powers	Judi
Pardon	(Foot-mat)
Convicted person	(ear) me wicket dalna
Advisory opinion	Advertisement
Supreme Court	Supreme chair

Visualisation: President APJ Abdul Kalam is making his **judi** standing on a **paye dan** and **puts wicket in his kan (ear).** He is **advertising** himself sitting on a **Supreme Chair**. You may or may not accept whatever he wants to say through this advertisement.

III. Legislative Powers

The President summons the sessions of both the houses of Parliament and prorogues them. He can even dissolve the Lok Sabha. These powers are formal and the President while using his powers must act according to the advice of the Council of Ministers headed by the Prime Minister. He inaugurates Parliament by addressing it after the general elections and also at the

outline the policies of the government.

A bill that the parliament is not in session and the government considers it necessary to have a law, the president can promulgate ordinances. These ordinances are submitted to the parliament at its next session. They remain valid for not more than six weeks from the date the parliament is convened unless approved by it earlier. The President permits the annual budget to be laid before the Lok Sabha. He recommends the introduction of money bills in the Lok Sabha.

Word	PMS
Summons	sums (addition)
Both	2 houses
Prorogues	(read)
Dissolve	dissolve
Loksabha	
Prime minister	Manmohan Singh
Inaugurates	cutting a ribbon
Parliament	Parliament house
Addressing	addressing
General election	general contesting for election
First session (1) every year	sun
Policies of govt.	Police
Bill	bill
Assent	cent
Promulgate	pomegranate
Ordinance	
Six weeks	vicks
Annual budget	Anu sitting on a bad shaped Jat

Visualisation: Visualise APJ Abdul Kalam with   legs (with lying legs) but still in power. He is giving **sums** to both the houses and asking them *padho padho* (read read). He dissolve the people of they are not working and sitting in *sabha* he is advicing them with the help of Manmohan singh

Now see, he is inaugurating the Parliament house by **cutting a ribbon** and addressing the generals who are contesting for the election and advising them to hold a **Sun** in their hands and if they don't do so he may give them to **police**.

After this, parliament is passing a bill to APJ Abdul Kalam which shows all the expenditures and wants APJ to spray **cent** on it, but he doesn't send him back to the parliament, parliament is again sending it back to APJ Abdul Kalam. Now when it has come for second time he gives his **cent** to it.

The days when the parliament is not in session, APJ Abdul Kalam can eat pomegranate, wearing an *odhni*. This *odhni* is submitted to the parliament when it gets opened. He eats pomegranate only with **vicks**. Whatever he eats, tells everything to Annu who is sitting on a jat and gives it to the *logo ki sabha*, where APJ Abdul Kalam asks for the bill.

IV. Emergency Powers

The president has certain emergency powers to meet abnormal or extraordinary situations. In

kinds of emergencies –
   i. Caused by war or aggression or armed rebellion.
   ii. Arising out of the failure of constitutional machinery in a state.

PMS

Word	PMS
Emergency power	emergency break
Abnormal	abnormal man
Constitutional	institution
Credit	credit card

Visualisation: Visualise APJ Abdul Kalam is driving a car, he puts emergency break as soon as he sees an abnormal person walking on the road. He is having three kinds of emergency break in his car. He uses these breaks whenever he sees war, which is due to an aggression or armed rebellion. If the break fails, he goes to an institution to get his machinery checked and give a

Chapter 4

SOME IMPORTANT FACTS RELATED TO GEOGRAPHY

1. The visible yellow face of the sun is called – photosphere
   PMS –
   photpsphere – photo of sphere

Visualisation: Visualise that you see a **yellow sphere on the surface of the sun** and you are taking the **photo of the sphere**.

2. Planetry winds consists of – Trade winds
   PMS –
   Planetry – planet
   Trade – traders

Visualisation: Visualise that on a planet there are lot of traders who sell winds.

3. The atmospheric layer closest to the earth is called – Troposphere
   PMS –
   Troposphere – top – sphere

Visualisation: Visualise that a **top shaped like sphere** by spinning, is pulling **the atmospheric layer closer to the earth**.

4. The sun's energy is called – Insolation
   PMS –
   Insolation – in – sole – lotion

Visualisation: Visualise that you are taking some **energy from the sun** this energy on the **sole of your shoes with a lotion**.

5. Kushinagar is known for – the place where Lord Buddha breathed his last.
   PMS –
   Kushinagar – Khusi (happy)

Visualisation: Visualise that Buddha (old man) breaths his last and the people of that city are having a lot of *khusi* (happiness).

TO MEMORISE IMPORTANT CANALS

Examples:

1. Kiel canal – between London & beltic parts.

   PMS –

Keil canal	keel (pin)
London	lawn & don
Baltic	(bucket)

Visualisation: Visualise that in a **canal** there are big **keels (pins)** and you are collecting these keels in a *balti* (bucket) and taking them to the **don sitting** in **a lawn**.

   PMS –

Panama	– (mango)
Atlantic	at lawn
	(throwing paise)

Visualisation: Visualise that you are eating *Paan* and *Aam* (**mango) in a lawn** and then you start **throwing** *paisa* **in an ocean**.

IMPORTANT NATURAL LAKES

Examples:

Name	Location
Great Bear	Canada
Baikal	Russia
PMS:	
Great Bear	great bear
Canada	can
Baikal	bike
Russsia	(rope)

Visualisation: Visualise that a **great bear** is taking a **can** of a cold drink.

Visualise that you are pulling your **bike** with the help of a *rassi* (rope).

IMPORTANT CITIES OF THE WORLD

Examples:

City	location
Abadan	Iran
Havana	Cuba
PMS:	
Abadan	a bad – don (see gulshan grover as bad man)
Iran	rain
Havana	(wind)
Cube	ice cube

Visualisation: Visualise that a **bad don** is standing in the **rain**, that an **ice cube hava (wind)**.

MEMORISING SOME GEOGRAPHICAL TERMS

make a suitable link.

Examples:

1. **Altiplano:** A high plane in the Andes mountains.
2. **Basin:** An extensive hollow in the earth's crust.
3. **Estuary:** Funnel-shaped mouth of a river caused by the shrinking of the lower part of the river valley.
4. **Lianos:** The vast tropical grasslands, north to the equatorial forests of the Amazo basin.
5. **Taiga:** A belt of coniferous forests of the northern hemisphere.

1. **PMS:**

    Altiplano   all – tea – plane

    Andes   ande (eggs)

Visualisation: Visualise all people in a **plane** are **taking tea** with **ande (eggs)**.

2. **PMS:**

    Basin   besan

Visualisation: Visualise that you are plugging the **hollow part of the earth** with **besan**.

3. **PMS:**

    Estuary   ass – tree

Visualisation: An ass sees that the lower part of a river valley is shrinking to the shape of the tunnel, so he climbs on the tree.

4. **PMS:**

    Lianos

    Tropical   topi (cap)

    Amazon   maze

Visualisation: Visualise that a **lioness** goes in a vast **grassland** with a *topi* on her head and **maze**.

5. PMS:

    Taiga   tanga

    Coniferous   conference

    Northern

    Hemisphere   spherical room

Visualisation: Visualise that you are pulling a *tanga* with your belt into forests where a conference is going on in a spherical room which is being attended by a *nari*.

GEOGRAPHY LONG THEORY

Question: Write a short note on drainage system.

Answer: The Himalayan and Peninsular Rivers may be divided into a number of drainage and basins. The rivers originating in the Himalayans consist of three river system.

They are:

1. The Indus System
2. The Ganga System
3. The Brahmputra system

These river systems constitute two main drainage basins – the Indus and the Ganga Brahmputra

The Indus sytem: The Indus rises in Tibet near the Mansarovar lake. Flowing west and north-westwards, it enters the Indian territory in Jammu & Kashmir. It forms a picturesque gorge in this part. Several tributaries – Zaskar, Shyok, Nubra, and Hunza join it in the Kashmir Region.

reaches the Arabian sea, east of Karachi. The Indus Plain has a very gentle slope. With a total length about 2900 km, the Indus is one of the longest rivers of the world. Little over one third of the Indus basin is located in India (Jammu & Kashmir, Himachal Pradesh and Punjab. With regard to the sharing of the Indus water, there is treaty between India and Pakistan. According to the regulations of the Indus water treaty, India can use only 20 percent of the total water carried by this river system. We use the waters of this river system to irrigate Punjab, Haryana and western parts of Rajasthan.

be as follows:

Now pick the keywords from this Indus system and make their PMS as follows:

Word	PMS
Indus	Indu (a girl)
Tibet	Tibet
Mansarovar	man sitting near sarovar
West	watch
Northwest	nail – watch
Jammu and Kashmir	J & K
Picturesque gorge	picture – George Bush
Tributaries	3 boots
Zaskar	Jassi in car
Shy ok	shy o.k
Nabru	(wearing loosen clothes)
Hunza	(Tv actress in Khichdi)
Ladhak	(a boy)
Baltistan	(bucket)
Gilgit	(chameleon)
Attock	a talk
Mithankot	(sweets)
Southwards	
Pakistan	Parvez Musharaff
Arabian sea	an Arabian
East of Karachi	eggs in Karahi
2900 km	nib
Indus Basin	Indu – wash basin
Himachal Pradesh	Hema
Treaty	treat
20 %	bat and ball (phonetic code)
Plain	plane
Basin	wash basin
Haryana	(every man)
Western part of Rajasthan	watch Havamahal

Comprehensive Memory Development Course

Visualisation: Indu is coming from **Tibet**, from there she sees a **man sitting near a** *sarovar* putting his head in a lake. Indu asks him what he is doing; he says **his watch** the lake and the **watch** will reach in **nail** and this nail opens in Jammu and Kashmir, and if it reaches J & K, it will come in **pictures**, as this watch is of **George Bush**.

Indu now takes **3 boots** and ask that man to take these 3 boots to **Jassi**, who is sitting in the **car** in **shyness**, saying **ok**; he went there & he saw a *Jhabru* who is looking like Hansa, one who is in Khichdi, going to Kashmir.

Hansa is taking a *ladka* who is carrying a *balti* with a *girgit* inside and she is saying we are going for **a talk** to Kashmir.

There they will also collect water from 5 rivers of the Punjab (you can easily mention 5 rivers here) and will get free *mithai* from Indu there, as she is going to join us there.

Now visualise Indu is wearing a *sari* going to meet **Pervez Musharaff**, with him is sitting an **Arabian girl**, eating eggs.

Now Indu is taking a **plane** and starting this plane with the help of a **nib**; now she is crossing the biggest river of the world. Now she goes to the **basin** to wash her hands, where she sees **Hema** showing her   and saying she is the queen of Jammu & Kashmir.

The water from the basin is going to be shared by India and Pakistan, which is going to be a treat from Indu to them.

In this treat **bat and ball** will be distributed by India. India is going to use this bat and ball to irrigate. **Watch** in **Havamahal** where *har aadmi* is having a big   to irrigate.

This is how you can visualise the whole Indus drainage system.

The Ganga System: The Ganga acquires its name after it's two headstreams – the Alaknanda and the Bhagirathi join at Devprayag. The Ganga enters the plains from the Himalayas at Hardwar. It is joined by a large number of tributaries from the north. Among them, the Ghaghara, the Gandak, and the Kosi enter the northern potential plains of India from Nepal. These rivers have tremendous potential to generate waterpower and to irrigate lands both in Nepal and India. By mutual trust and cooperation, the sharing of river water for development purposes can usher in prosperity to the people of both the countries.

The Yamuna and the Son are the two main right bank tributaries of the Ganga. Find out the

– southeast and enters Bangladesh as Padma. A bifurcation channel of the mainstream, called the Bhagirathi – Hooghly runs southwards through the deltaic plain to the Bay of Bengal. The

known as the Jamuna here. Further down it receives the Meghna the Bay of Bengal. There is a treaty between India and Bangladesh with regard to the sharing of the Ganga water.

The length of the Ganga is over 2500 km. in India, it has the largest Basin. The Ganga river system drains most of north India.

PMS

Word	PMS
Ganga	Kiran Juneja (Mahabharat)
Alaknanda	Alka
Bhagirathi	
Devprayag	Devanand
Plains	Plane
Tributaries	3 boots
North	Nail
Ghagra	(Rajasthani dress)
Gandak	
Kosi	(warm water)
Yamuna	(blackberries)
Son	See your son or your brother
Farraka	Frock
East – south east	Egg – sari
Bangladesh	Bangles
Padma	
Bhagirathi – hoogly	
Deltaplain	Dalda
Bay of Bengal	Paid to a tiger

Visualisation: Kiran Juneja on her head sees 2 things – **Alka** and a *rath*. Now **Alka bhagi** (runs) with a *rath* to Devanand as she loves him. They took the **plane** from there, went to **Haridwar** and got married, suddenly **3 boots** were thrown from a **nail**, there was **genda** wearing a *ghagra* and the water in which he was standing was **Kosa**. Then this **genda** went through the **nali** to **Nepal**.

Now visualise Kiran Juneja is starting a generator and with the help of which waterpower will increase and this water will be used for irrigating the lands of Nepal and India.

Now see **Kiran Juneja** has opened a bank in which your **son** (or brother) is sitting and eating *jamun*.

Kiran had got lot of money from bank; so she is going to buy **eggs**, which are wrapped in a *sari*; she is also taking **bangles** as she wants to look like **Padma Khanna**.

Now Kiran Juneja is ready, but standing on a path which is bifurcated. She runs with the help of a **Rath** beating the **horse with a hook wearing a sari**, eating **dalda** and for this she paid to a tiger.

As she became **Padma**, she wears s**ari and bangles** and joins **Brahma** and his *putra* (son) eating *jamuns*, further when she moves meets **Meghnath**, who killed the **tiger of Bengal**.

Length of Ganga – 2500 km – length of the **Bindi** Kiran Juneja is wearing, is lengthy as a **nail** and she is washing her face in the **largest basin** in IndIa.

The Brahmputra system: The Brahmaputra originates in Tibet very close to the source of the Indus and Satluj. It is slightly longer than the Indus, but most of its course lies outside India. It

around it and enters Arunachal Pradesh of India. The undercutting done by this mighty river is

joined by several tributaries. The river in Tibet is known as Tsangpo.

Here the river receives less volume of water and has less slit. But in India, it passes through a region, which receives heavy rainfall. As such the river carries a large volume of water and considerable amount of slit. The Brahmputra has a braided channel in most its length in Assam, with the channel.

The sifting of channels of the river is also very common. The fury of the river during rains is

The main watershed in the Peninsular India is formed by the Western Ghats, which is in close proximity to the western coast. Most of the major rivers of the Peninsula such as the Mahanadi,

basins of the peninsular rivers are comparatively small in size.

Word	PMS
Brahamaputra	Brahma Putra
Indus	Indu
Satluj	Sat-lodge
Eastward	Egg
Namcha Barwa	Nacha (Dance) in Bar
7757	Cake/Lake
Arunachal Pradesh	Arun
5,500	Lily, 00
Assam	Tea
Tributaries	3 But
Tsangpo	Tarzan

Braided channel	Beard
Peninsula	Pen
Mahanadi	Visualise Nadi k Uper Nadi
Godavari	Goad me
Krishna	Krishna Bhagwan
Kaveri	(Crow)
Delta	Dalda (Oil)
Narmada	Nar + Mada (Male Female)
Tapti	Tapti hue (Hot)

Mental Picture: Visualise **Brahma** and his **putra** (son) playing on Tibet with **Indu** outside a **lodge**, also eating **eggs**. When you reach there you see people **dancing outside the bar** eating **cake** near the **lake** from there you take U-turn, you see your friend **Arun** is asking you to join him to a river, nearby where **Lily** is waiting for them. You are refusing saying that you have already given them to Tarzan, and his father Brahma who has a big beard, and a business of tea selling.

Now you are sitting near a river and writing with a **pen** suddenly you see **Krishna** swimming in the **nadi** (river) carrying a   in his **goad**   **egg** where
        Tiger, seeing the Tiger, Krishna's mouth is closed by **Dalda**. He turns backward and **watch**; there he meets **Nar and Mada** sitting on a **Tapti (hot)**

TO MEMORISE GEOGRAPHICAL MAPS

Steps to memorise: The method to memorise the map is called GRID METHOD.

    (ii). This should be done with very light hand.
(3) Now with the help of "Mnemonic Pen" see the code, each square is having a code" like:
       00   -   Sauce
       01   -   Tie
       02   -   Eno
       03   -   Ma
       04   -   Ray
       05   -   Hall
(4) Also visualise each square, as a room, having an opening from its left side centre, as

Example:
 (a) Now in room 01, i.e., you have to associate tie with gold.

(b) Ma with iron ore

Visualisation: now here you are not able to visualise "iron ore"; for this you can use PMS of iron ore. It can be an "iron" with which we iron our cloths.

Now mentally associate Ma with iron. Visualise Ma is ironing your cloths, just in front of the door, near to the wall.

(c) 25 and coco

Code of 25 is Nail and coco

Visualisation: visualise lot of coco, on each coco see a nail.

(d) Next is 31 with lead and zinc code for 31 is Mat

PMS for lead + zinc; see lot of lead pencils in a Zen car.

Visualisation: Visualise that your mat is full of lead pencis and you are putting this mat in a Zen car which is on the left corner of his room. Also visualise 31 with tin. So mat with tin. Visualise that you are putting rolled mats with tin; you are placing this tin just on the right hand of the door.

(e) 33 and lead + zinc

Code for 33 is Mama

PMS for lead and zinc is lead pencils in Zen.

Visualisation: as we have proposed earlier, so now make a mental picture that your   is throwing all the lead pencils in the Zen car which is parked in the centre of the room.

(f) 42 and manganese

Code for 42 is rain

PMS for magnese is mangoes

Visualisation: Visualise that it is raining heavily outside and you are plucking the mangoes from a mango tree and putting on the left side of the room, just adjacent of the side wall. (Please see tha placement in the map)

(g) See in room no. 38

You have to link 38 with silver

You have to link 38 with lead and zinc

You have to link 38 with gold

PMS for silver: you can see any silver ornament.

PMS for lead+ zinc: you can see lead pencils in the Zen.

PMS for Gold: you can see any gold ornament.

Now visualise:

See silver ornaments are placed just in front of the room's door.

ornaments and runs away.

pencils from the room, put them in a Zen car, which is parked on the left side of the room just adjacent to the centre of the left wall.

from the extreme left corner of the room & runs away.

(h) See block – 72 and wheat

Code for 72 is can

PMS for wheat is actual wheat

Visualisation: A very big can of wheat which is touching the roof, now in the centre, but little right side of the room.

(i) 73 and copper

Code for 73 is comb

PMS for copper is copper utensils

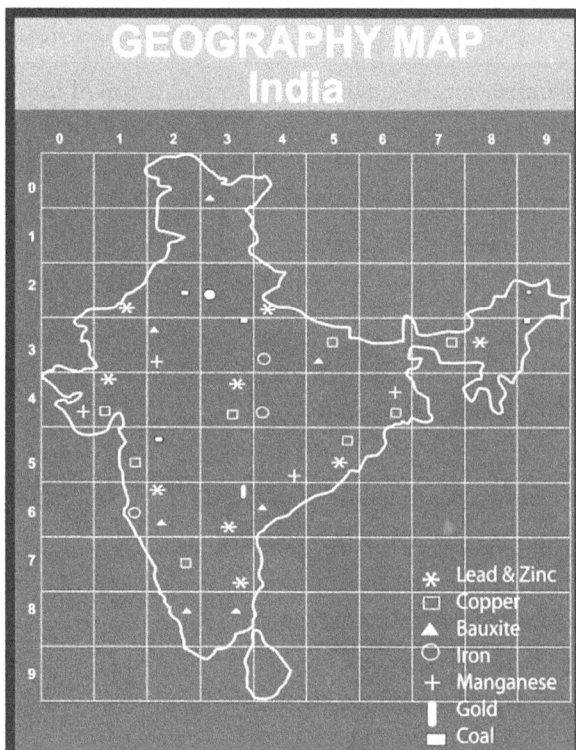

Visualisation: Visualise that comb are kept in copper utensils. The utensils are placed in 3 parts of the room – one in the centre of the room, other one on the left side of the door and one on the right side of the room.

In the same way, as we have learnt to memorise minerals in South America, we can use the same method to memorise anything in the map. We can learn – mountains, rivers, ores, centuries, national parks and crops, etc.

Comprehensive Memory Development Course

Chapter 5

MEMORISING LAWS

1. The Features of A Company

>Separate Legal Entity
>Perpetual Succession
>Common Seal

Visualisaton: Visualise anyone of your companions (Company). He is wearing a mask

(perpetual succession), when walks, leaving his footprints ((Common seal).

2. The existence of the company doesn't come to an end even if all the members of company die since one of the characteristics of the company is 'perpetual succession'

Visualisation: 'Perpetual Succession' (puppet plays the role of members in a company).

3. A Private company can't accept deposits from the public or any person other than its members, directors or their relatives; this would amount to conversion of private company in to a public company by default.

Visualisation: In a private car only its **Driver (Director)**, or their relatives, or mummy (members) can **sit (deposit)**, public is not allowed to **sit (deposit)**, as it would amount into conversion of a private car into a public car.

4. Effects of Incorporation

>A company becomes a body corporate
>Acquires legal recognition
>Gets a name
>Comes into existence from such date
>Objects of the company are laid down

Visualisation:

when baby borns –   (Laid objectives).

    5. Duties of A Promoter

             Full & fair disclosure of interest

Remedies to companies against promoters

             Rescinding of contract

             Suit for breach of trust

Visualisation: A person named **PRAMOD (Promoter)** started his **duty (Duties)** in a company,

                                    rescinded his contract of
duty; searched out his   **breach of trust**.

To memorise sections / sub-sections

call himself a genius. So, now we are going to help you in memorising these sections and subsections. You are requested to follow the rules and regulations. Try to use all the laws of memory, i.e. law of association, law of visualisation and law of ridiculus thinking. These laws will help you in learning/ memorising things at a much faster rate.

Section	Relating to...
252	Minimum number of directors
274	
295	Loans to directors
471	Effect of winding up order
500	Meeting of creditors
571	Notice to customers on registeration of banking company with limited liability
142	Penalties
147	Publication of name by company
175	Chairman of meeting
217	Board's report
220	
234	Power of register to call for information or explanation
240	Production of document and evidence
372	Purchase by the company of shares, etc., of other companies
385	Certain persons not to be appointed as managers

Comprehensive Memory Development Course

Now we make the PMS of the section number and take out a keyword from the statement and make their PMS. Now link them together and properly visualise it, once you visualise it, you will not forget what statement lies in a particular section.

1. Section 252 – minimum number of directors

   PMS –

252	nylon
Minimum	mini skirt

Visualisation: Visualise the directors are wearing **mini skirts** tied with **nylon** wire.

   PMS –

274	Nikker

Visualisation: Visualise all the directors wearing **nikker** are   .

3. Section 295 – loans to directors, etc.

   PMS –

295	Nipple
loans	lawns

Visualisation: Visualise all the directors are stting in the **lawn** and are sucking **nipples**.

4. Section 471 – Effect of winding up order

   PMS –

471	Badminton Racket

Visualisation: Visualise that after playing badminton you are **winding** up the racket and other items.

5. Section 500 – Meeting of creditors

   PMS –

500	Lassi
Creditors	Credit card

Visualisation: Visualise that in a meeting you are buying **lassi** showing the **credit card**.

6. Section 571 – Notice to customers on registration on banking company with limited liability

   PMS –

571	locket

Visualisation: Visualise that a company is sending a notice written on a **locket** to all his customers.

7. Section 142 – penalties

   PMS –

142	train

Visualistaion: Visualise that you have entered into a train without ticket and you are paying penalty.

8. Section 175 – Publicaton of name by company

   PMS –

   147   Truck

Visualisation: Visualise that Truck is a name of the publication given by a company.

9. Section 175 – Chairman of a meeting

   PMS:

   175

Visualisation: Visualise a scene of meeting, all men sitting on the chair are *takla* (bald).

10. Section 217 – Board's report

    PMS –

    217

Visualisation: Visualise that you are in class room writing the report of the *natak* you saw last time.

Chapter 6

MEMORISING IMPORTANT FACTS OF THE PHYSICS

1. The unit of energy is - Joule

   PMS –

Energy	energetic people
Joule	(net)

Visualisation: Visualise that you are trapping **energetic people** into a *jaal* (net) and they are struggling for coming out of it.

2. Stress has the dimensions of ML -1 T -2

   PMS –

Dimension	men are dying
MLT	melt
	1 sun
	2 shoe

Visualisation: Visualise that so many **men** are **melting** and **dying** because they are in **stress** near **sun** while **wearing shoes**.

3. What is the SI unit of Planck's constant? - Joule second

   PMS –

SI	Sai Baba
Joule	(net)
Planck	((bed)
Unit	knitting

Visualisation: Sai Baba got second prize for **knitting jaal** on **palang**.

4. A bomb explodes into a large number of tiny fragments. The total momentum of all the fragments is zero

   PMS –

Zero	hero

Visualisation: Visualise that a bomb explodes into a large numbers of tiny fragments and these fragments are caught by a **hero**.

PMS –

Kinetic   Kinetic Honda

Visualisation: Visualise that if you buy less than 1 **kinetic Honda**

6. Two forces of equal magnitude have a resultant whose magnitude is equal to that of either force. What is the angle between the two forces? – 120 degree
   PMS –

   120 degree   dance (1-d, 2- n, 0- s) (phonetic code)
   Magnitude   Meghna (a girl)

Visualisation: Visualise that **Meghnas** (visualise two similar girls) are standing and a new Meghna emerges from the mid of the two Meghnas, who is **dancing**.

7. What is the SI unit of magnetic permeability? – Henry per metre
   PMS –

   SI   Sai Baba
   Permeability   pummed hair
   Henry per metre   hen and meter

Visualisation: Visualise that Sai Baba has rolled magnets to **perm** his hair and beating a **hen with a meter**.

8. The most suitable metal for making permanent magnets is – steel

Visualisation: Visualise that you have got a **permanent magnet** that is made of **steel**.

9. Transformers are used in – AC circuits alone
   PMS –

   Ac   air conditioner

Visualisation: Visualise that your air conditioner is working on transformer instead of stabilizer.

10. Who discovered natural radioactivity? – Henry Becquerel
    PMS –

    Radioactivity   radio
    Henri Becquerel   hen who is quarreling

Visualisation: Make a visualisation that a **hen is quarreling** sitting on a **radio**.

11. Cadmium rods are used in a nuclear reactor for – 931 MeV
    PMS –

    Cadmium   cat

Rods	rod
Nuclear	nuclear furnace
931	PMT students (9=p, M=3, 1=t)

Visualisation: Visualise that **PMT students** are sitting on a **nuclear furnace**, **beating a cat** with a **rod**.

12. An aeroplane takes off the angle 'e' with the horizontal run-way. If the component of its velocity along the run way is v, what is the actual velocity? – v/cos e

    PMS –

v	vicks
cos	cosco ball
v/cose	we read it 'v' over 'cos e'

Visualisation: when an aeroplane takes off we apply **vicks** over **cosco ball**.

13. What is the value of acceleration due to gravity on the planet's surface?
    – 2ms2

    PMS –

Gravity	gravy
Planet	plate
2ms2 –	to miss having shoe

Visualisation: Visualise that you are putting **gravy** in a plate of only **to miss** having shoes.

14. The dimensions of angular momentum are – ML2 T-2

    PMS –

Angular	angry
Momentum	momento
Dimension	dying men
Ml -2	meal (having 2 times)
T -2	tea (twice)

Visualisation: Visualise that the dying men are angry and they are giving meal (twice) and tea (twice) as momento to all.

15. What is the SI Unit of Force Constant K? – NM -1

    PMS –

SI	Sai Baba
Force	forcefully
Constant	constantly
K	kite
NM -1	neem – on sun

Visualisation: Visualise that **Sai baba** _____ **kite forcefully** and **constantly** so that his kite could reach to the **neem** leaves which are on the **sun**.

MEMORISING SHORT TYPE QUESTIONS (WITH EXAMPLES)

1. What do you understand by the term, potential at a point?

   _____ that point.

   PMS –

Potential	pot (is in static state)
Point	see
Positive	doctor (+)

Visualisation: On a **pot** you put a **bindi** and carry it for a **doctor**. He puts it in the opposite (against) _____ **far away** to another bindi.

2. What do you understand by the E. M. F. of a cell?

Ans: Electromotive force. (E.M.F.) of a cell is potential difference across the terminal of the cell when the cell is in an open circuit, i.e. when no current is drawn from the cell.

   PMS –

E.M.F.	Electrons are in motion forcefully
potential difference	the change or difference in pot
cell terminal	terminal end of the cell
open circuit	open wire (not connected with electricity)

Visualisation: Visualise that electrons are in motion forcefully because of the **difference in pot** and it occurs only when the **terminal end of the cell** is not connected with **electricity**.

3. What do you mean by the sensitivty of potentiometer?

Ans: The sensititvity of potentiometer is the smallest potential difference.

   PMS –

Sensitivity	sensitive
Potentiometer	pot with meter
Smallest potential	small size pot
Difference	change

Visualisation: Visualise that there is a sensitive pot with meter but it is of the smallest size. And it changes when it is measured.

Comprehensive Memory Development Course

1. Conductor: A material in which electrons are relatively free to move.

   PMS –

Conductor	bus conductor
Electron	electrol

Visualisation: Visualise a **bus conductor** wearing a dress material on which **electron** packets are stuck, which he is distributing free with the ticket.

2. Capacitor: Any two conductors separated by an insulator to form solid state without passing through liquid state

   PMS –

Conductor	bus conductor
Insulator	sula (sleep)

Visualisation: Visualise that two **bus conductors** are sleeping and they can be separated by the different styles of their caps.

3. Colourimetry: Subject which deals with measurement of heat.

   PMS –

Colourimetry	coloured meter

Visualisation: Visualise that you are measuring heat, standing under the sun, with the help of a coloured meter.

4. Thermal capacity: The amount of heat required to raise the temperature of the whole body through 1 degree Celsius.

   PMS –

Whole body	your full body
1 degree Celsius	sun (rhyme)

Visualisation: Visualise that to rise the temperature of your body you are pouring heat with the help of thermos from the sun.

5. Volt

   The potential difference between two points.

   PMS –

Volt	Voltas refrigerator
Potential	pot cell
Two point	Two pants

Visualisation: I kept two pants and a cell in a pot and put them in a voltas refrigerator.

To memorise the properties of the plastic

Order	PMS	Visualisation
1. Sun	Light in weight	A sun made of plastic is light in weight
2. Shoe	Thermal and electric insulation	A plastic shoe has good thermal and electric insulation
3. Tree	Corrosion resistance	If plastic is applied to a tree it will not have corrosion
4. Door	Easy workability	A plastic door is easily workable or moveable
5. Knife	Adhesiveness	A plastic knife is used to apply adhesive
6. Vicks	Low fabrication cost into desired shapes	If vicks is applied to plastic, it can be made into desired shapes
7. Heaven	Decorative surface effect	Heaven is being decorated with plastic
8. Plate	Easy moulding	A plastic plate can be easily moulded into a cup
9. Wine	Insect resisitance	If wine is kept in plastic bottles, it becomes insect resisitance
10. Hen	Low thermal expansion	If a hen is made of plastic its thermal expansion will be low
11. Stick	Chemical intensive	A plastic stick is made of intensive chemical
12. Duck	Transparency	A plastic duck is transparent
13. Heart	Low maintenance cost	A heart made of plastic can be maintained at low cost
14. Chair	Low melting points	A plastic chair melts very easily at low temeperature
15. Hook	High refractive index	A plastic hook is highly refractive

To memorise the defect of vision

Summary: defect of vision and their correction

	Type of defect	Effect of defect	Correction
1.	Hypermetropia (long sightedness)	Nearby objects not clearly visible	By using convex lens of suitable power
2.	Myopia (short sightedness)	Distant objects are not clearly visible	By using concave lens of suitable power
3.	Astigmatism	Straight – line looks curved	Cylindercal lenses

PMS –

Type – *myopia*

"*my pia* (lover) is short sighted" (short sightedness)

Effect – distant objects are not clearly visible

"he cannot see me if I am standing far away"

Correction – by using concave lens of suitable power

"so he wants me to live inside a cave with him till the power of his eyes come back."

Visualisation: My *pia* is short sighted. He cannot see me if I am standing far away. So he wants me to live inside a cave with him till the power of his eyes come back.

Once this is learnt, a student will automatically learn **hypermertropia because it is very simple; just opposite to myopia**.

To memorise light year

We know that light year is the distance travelled by light in one year. But we often confuse its value. Here is how, we can learn it with the help of the memory method.

One light year = 9.46×10^{12} km

PMS –

9.46	brg (bridge) (g is silent)
12	duck

Visualisation: Visualise that there is a long **bridge** and 10 ducks have been crossing it for a year and still they have to go a long way to cross it.

To memorise the relation between Newton and Dyne

Newton – 10 to the power 5 dyne

PMS –

Newton	Newton
10	hen
5	knife
Dyne	dinner

Visualisation: Visualise that **Newton** is cutting a **hen** with a **knife** because he wanted to have it for **dinner**.

To memorise physics formulae

1. Obtain the mathematical form of Joule's law regarding the heating effect of Electric current

   According to Ohm's law: $V = I R$

   V = Potential difference

   I = Current

R = Resistance

The Quantity of charge passing through the conductor in time 't' is given by –

Charge = Current x Time

Q = I x T

Work Done= W = Potential Difference x Charge

W = VQ

W = I^2 RT.

PMS and visualisation through cartoons instantly:

V = I R   Q = I T

VEERU never QuITs

W =   V   Q

The winner shows a V sign and gets the trophy from the Queen.

2. Joule's Law : H = I^2 RT.

PMS –

 H = Harbajan Singh

 I = he plays for India

 R = Right Hand off Spinner

 T = Tail ender batsman

3. F = BLI sin

PMS –

F	force of a current
Bli	(cat)
Sin	singing with its throat (theta)

Visualisation: Visualise that a   (cat) after receiving force by current tries to sing with its **throat** (sin).

4. De Broglie waves

   = h/ mv

PMS –

De Broglie waves = A dog is barking on waves of the sea

   = y is in opposite direction so see a yatcht (alphabet 'y' means) is hanged opposite in direction.

h/ mv = we will read it as h over mv, visualise that all hens (h) are sitting over moov (mv)

Visualisation: A dog is barking on the waves of the sea, suddenly it sees **a yacht** is going in the opposite direction, (it is hanged) and on the yacht there are hens, and **all hens are sitting over moov ointment**.

Chapter 7

MEMORISING PERIODIC TABLE

There are 108 elements in the modern periodic table. The students of Chemistry are required to memorise these elements. Generally, the elements can't be picturised/ visualised. So we can make PMSs for these elements, as under:

ELEMENTS	PMS
1) Hydrogen (H)	Hydrogen balloon
2) Helium (He)	Helen (Actress)
3) Lithium (Li)	Lichee
4) Beryllium (Be)	Borolene (cream)
5) Boron (B)	Bora (sack)
6) Carbon (C)	Car
7) Nitrogen (N)	Night
8) Oxygen (O)	Ox
9) Fluorine (F)	Floor
10) Neon (Ne)	knees
11) Sodium (Na)	Soda bottle
12) Magnesium (Mg)	Maggie
13) Aluminium (Al)	Aaloo
14) Silicon (Si)	Sita maa
15) Phosphorus (P)	Fox with pores
16) Sulphur (S)	Sulpha
17) Chlorine (Cl)	Clown
18) Argon (Ar)	Gun
19) Potassium (K)	Pot
20) Calcium (Ca)	Calcium tablet

21) Scandium (Sc)	Scan
22) Titanium (Ti)	Titanic ship
23) Vanadium (V)	Van
24) Chromium (Cr)	Crow
25) Magenese (Mn)	Mango
26) Iron (Fe)	Iron
27) Cobalt (Co)	Bolt
28) Nickel (Ni)	Knicker
29) Copper (Cu)	Cup
30) Zinc (Zn)	Zin
31) Gallium (Ga)	Gali
32) Germanium (Ge)	Jam
33) Arsenic (As)	Sainic (Sainik)
34) Selenium (Se)	Saloon
35) Bromine (Br)	Broom
36) Krypton (Kr)	Cry
37) Rubidium (Rb)	Rubi Bhatia
38) Strontium (Sr)	Strong
39) Yttrium (Y)	Team
40) Zirconium (Zr)	Jerk
41) Niobium (Nb)	New bomb
42) Molybdenium (Mo)	Mobile
43) Technetium (Tc)	Technician
44) Ruthenium (Ru)	Rath
45) Rhodium (Rh)	Road
46) Palladium (Pd)	Paddle
47) Silver (Ag)	Silver
48) Cadmium (Cd)	Candle
49) Indium (In)	Indian
50) Tin (Sn)	Tin
51) Antimony (Sb)	Aunty
52) Tellurium (Te)	Telcum powder
53) Iodine (I)	Iodex
54) Xenon (Xe)	Zeenat Aman (actress)
55) Caesium (Cs)	Scissors

56) Barium (Ba)	Bar
57) Lanthanum (La)	Lantern
58) Cerium (Ce)	Saari
59) Praseodymium (Pr)	Prasad
60) Neodymium (Nd)	New+dam
61) Promrehium (Pm)	Rome
62) Samarium (Sm)	Marium (Mother of Jesus)
63) Europium (Eu)	Europe
64) Gadolinium (Gd)	Gadar movie
65) Terbium (Tb)	Turbine
66) Dysprosium (Dy)	Disprin
67) Holmium (Ho)	Hole
68) Erbium (Er)	Erbi (Arbi - language)
69) Thulium (Tm)	Hulia (in Hindi)
70) Ytterbium (Yb)	Yatri+bomb
71) Lutetium (Lu)	Loot
72) Hafnium (Hf)	Half+knee
73) Tantalum (Ta)	Tent
74) Tungsten (W)	Tongue
75) Rhenium (Re)	Rainy
76) Osmium (Os)	Osho (Indian philosopher)
77) Iridium (Ir)	Ride
78) Platinum (Pt)	Plate
79) Gold (Au)	Gold
80) Mercury (Hg)	Mercury bulb
81) Thallium (Tl)	Thal (big plate)
82) Lead (Pb)	Lead pencil
83) Bismuth (Bi)	Biscuit
84) Polonium (Po)	Pole
85) Astatine (At)	State
86) Radon (Ra)	Don
87) Francium (Fr)	France
88) Radium (Ra)	Radio
89) Actinium (Ac)	Acting
90) Thorium (Th)	Theory

91) Protactinium (Pa)	Protect
92) Uranium (U)	Uranium bomb
93) Neptunium (Np)	Neptune (planet)
94) Plutonium (Pu)	Pluto planet
95) Americium (Am)	America
96) Curium (Cm)	M. Curi
97) Berkelium (Bk)	Berkel (scientist)
98) Californium (Cf)	California
99) Einsteinium (Es)	Einstein (scientist)
100) Fermium (Fm)	Farm house
101) Mendelevium (Md)	Mendeleev (scientist)
102) Nobelium (No)	Nobel Prize
103) Lawrencium (Lr)	Lawrencium (scientist)
104) Rutherfordium (Rf)	Rutherford (scientist)
104) Dubnium (Db)	Dabur
106) Seaborgium (Sg)	Seabirg (scientist)
107) Bohrium (Bh)	Bohr scientist
108) Hassium (Hs)	Hiss (Movie)

To memorise elements with their atomic numbers you can link elements with atomic numbers in anyway, we do not need to be logical. The more abnormal and funny the association is, the more memorable it will be.

After that, do revise the atomic numbers of the elements through visualisation two to three times, then appear for the exercise and check out your score.

FACTS TO REMEMBER (WITH SOME EXAMPLES)

1. Most ductile metal   Gold
2. Most reactive solid element   Li
3. Most reactive liquid element   Cs
4. Liquid metal   Hg, Ga, Cs, Fr
5. Metal with highest m.p   W
6. Element kept in water   P
7. Volatile d-block element   Zn, Cd, Hg
8. Highest ionisation potential   He
9. Lowest ionisation   Cs
10. First Nobel Prize in chemistry   Vant Haff
11. 3 period   Typical or bridge element

12.	Alkali metal	I A
13.	Alkaline earth metal	II A
14.	S-block + P-block	Representative elements, normal or Main Group element
15.	D-block	Transitional elements
16.	F block elements	Inner-transition, rare-earth elements
17.	IB elements (Cu, Ag, Au)	Coinage or currency
18.	K, Rb, Cs are used is photoelectric cells	Due to their low ionisation potential value.
19.	Flux + impurities	Slag
20.	Mg act as a bridge element between	II A and II B
21.	Na acts as a bridge for sub groups	IA and IB.
22.	Purest form of silica	Quarts
23.	Liquid non-metal	q Br_2
24.	Element with maximum number of allotropes	Tin (Sn)

In order to memorise the facts to remember, we need to make relations between them. If you remember these in a form of stories which has a personal meaning, you are more likely to remember it.

1. Most ductile metal — Gold

   Word — **PMS**

   Ductile — Duck + tiles

   Visualisation: Most of the **golden ducks** are walking on the **golden tiles**.

2. Most reactive solid element — Li

   Word — **PMS**

   Li (Lithium) — Lichee

   Visualisation: I am eating **solid lichee** to become **more active**.

3. Most reactive liquid element — Cs (Caesium)

   Word — **PMS**

   Cs (Caesium) — Scissors

   Visualisation: I am very **active**, I can cut **liquid** with the **scissors**.

4. Liquid metal — Hg + Ga + Cs + Fr

   Word — **PMS**

   Hg (Mercury) — Mercury bulb

   Ga (Gallium) — Gali

   Cs (Caesium) — Scissor

   Fr (Francium) — Frock

Visualisation: I am sitting in the **gali** under the **mercury bulb**, cutting **frock** with the **scissors** and throwing it into the **liquid**.

5. Metal with highest m.p   W (Tungsten)

Word	PMS
W (Tungsten)	Tongue
M.P (Melting point)	M.P (State)

Visualisation: My Tongue is of Metal, it is very high. It can reach up to M.P.

6. Element kept in water   P (Phosphorus)

Word	PMS

P (phosphorus fox with pores Visualisation: A **fox with pores** always want to live in **water**.

7. Volatile d–block element   Zn, Cd, Hg

Word	PMS
Zn (Zinc)	Zin
Cd (Cadmium)	Candle
Hg (Mercury)	Mercury bulb
Volatile	Vale + tie

Visualisation: A **zin** comes out from **mercury bulb**, takes **candle**, and goes inside the **vale** where he wears a **tie**.

8. Highest ionisation potential   He (Helium)

Word	PMS
He (Helium)	Helen
Ionisation potential	Energy require to peel the onion

Visualisation: When **helen** was **very small**, she required **more and more energy to peel the onion**.

9. Lowest ionisation potential   Cs (Caessium)

Word	PMS
Cs (Caessium)	Scissors
Ionisation potential	Energy required to peel the onion

Visualisation: I have a **big scissors**, so I require very **small energy to peel the onion** with the help of **big scissors**. It is easy to **peel the onion**.

10. First Nobel Prize in chemistry   Vant Haff

Word	PMS
Vant Haff	Want half

Visualisation: First, I want half of this **Nobel Prize** of **chemistry**.

11. 3 period   Typical or bridge element

Word	PMS
3	Three monkeys of Gandhiji

Visualisation: Three monekys of Gandhiji are making a **bridge** which is very **typical**.

12. Alkali metal   I A

Word	PMS
Alkali	Kali maa
I	Raja
A	Apple

Visualisation: Kali maa is giving **apple** to **raja** as prasad.

13. Alkaline earth metal   II A

Word	PMS
Alkaline	(Mattress)
II	Couple
A	Apple

Visualisation: Kaline is put on the **earth** and **couple** are sitting on it, and eating **apple**.

14. S – block + P – block   Representative, Normal, Main Group element

Word	PMS
S + p	S.P

Visualisation: S.P is the **main** man in his **group**, he is **normally representing** the **police**.

15. d-block   Transitional element

Word	PMS
Transitional	Transistor
D	Dog

Visualisation: My **dog** is listening to a **transistor**,

16. f–block element   Inner transitional, rare earth Element

Word	PMS
F	Fan
Transitional	Transistor

Visualisation: I **rarely** sit on the **earth** under the **fan**, wearing an **inner** for listening to a **transistor**.

17. I B element   Coinage or currency
(Cu, Ag, Au)

Word	PMS
I	Sun
B	Boy
Coinage	Coin

Cu (Copper)	Cup
Au (Gold)	Gold
Ag (Silver)	Silver

Visualisation: Golden Coin or **Currency** is falling from the **sun** and a **boy** the **cup**, which is shining like **silver**.

18. K, Rb, Cs are used in photoelectric cells due to their low ionisation potential value.

Word	PMS
K (Potassium)	Pot
Rb (Rubidium)	Ruby Bhatia
Cs (Caesium)	Scissors
Photo–electric cells	Photo + electricity
Ionisation potential	Energy required to peel the Onion

Visualisation: Ruby Bhatia requires **low energy to peel the onion**, and after peeling it with the **scissors**, she puts it into the **pot** and makes **photo** by passing **electricity**.

19. Flux + Impurities Slag

Word	PMS
Flux	Lux
Impurities	Impure
Slag	Leg

Visualisation: I am hitting **impure lux** with my **leg**.

20. Mg acts as a bridge element between IIA and IIB

Word	PMS
Mg (Magnesium)	Maggie
II	Zoo
A	Apple
B	Boy

Visualisation: A zoo is full of **apple** and the **boys** from other **zoo** want to reach there. So, they make a **bridge** with the help of long **maggie**.

22. Purest form of silica   Quartz

Word	PMS
Si (Silica)	Sita

Visualisation: Sita maa is wearing a **pure** form of **quartz** (wrist watch) in her hand.

23. Liquid non–metal   Br2

Word	PMS
Br (Bromine)	Broom
N.M (Non Metal)	Neem
2	Couple

Visualisation: Liquid is spreading around the **neem** and **couples** are cleaning it with **broom**.

24. Elements with maximum number of allotropes is tin

Word	PMS
Sn (Tin)	Tin
Allotropes	All + trophy
Visualisation:	**tin** with **all + trophy to maximum**.

FORMULAE OF IUPAC

In writing IUPAC name of an aliphatic compound the following sequence is followed.

For example:

$$\overset{2}{\underset{}{}}\ \overset{2}{\underset{|}{\text{N}\overset{}{\text{O}_2}}}\ \overset{2}{}$$

IUPAC name   —   3nitrobutane-1-amine

Word root   –   But

So, we will use chain and acronym method to get rid of this problem. It helps us to remember

WORD	ACRNYM METHOD	CODE
Secondary	S.P	(superintendent of police)
	P.P	(PaPpu)
Word root	W.R	WaR
	P.S	PuRse
	S.S	SaaS (mother-in-low)

I.U.P.A.C name: S.P is going to PAPPU to give the information of WAR, he opens a Big PURSE and shows papers to his SAAS.

QUANTUM NUMBERS

1. Principle quantum number
2. Azimuthal quantum number
3. Magnetic quantum number
4. Spin quantum number

words, then we will make a connection between them.

WORDS	PMS
Quantum	Queen
Principle	Principal
Azimuthal	Azi + mouth
Magnetic	Magnet
Spin	Pin

Visualisation: The QUEEN was walking with the PRINCIPAL. She said -- AZI in my MOUTH a MAGNET has got stucked, please bring it out with this PIN.

ENTROPY

Entropy (s) is a degree of randomness.

WORD	PMS
S	Son
Entropy	Trophy
Degree	Degree college
Randomness	Rain + dumb

Visualisation: In a DEGREE COLLEGE, it started RAINing and a DUMB person is hiding himself inside the TROPHY won by his SON.

In order to memorise it, we need to make a connection between them. If you memorise it in a form of story which has a personal meaning, you are more likely to remember it.

INCREASING ORDER OF ENTROPY

Solid   Liquid   Gas.

Word	**PMS**
Entropy	Trophy

Visualisation: **gas**, therefore, I buy a **trophy** which is full of **liquid**, i am drinking it, after that I become a like **solid** statue.

DIAGONAL RELATIONSHIP

Diagonal relationship arises due to:

Almost similar atomic sizes.

Almost similar electro negativities.

Almost similar polarising power of ions.

Almost similar ionisation energy.

In order to memorise these facts, we should make the funny associations to give them a permanent space in our memory.

WORD	PMS
Atomic	Atom bomb
Electronegativities	Electron + bad (-ve)
Polarising power (p.p)	Pappu (acronym method)
Ions	Onions
Ionisation energy	Energy required to peel the onion
Diagonal	Dragon

Visualisation: My RELATIONSHIP with DRAGON is very strong because we both have

ELECTRON became DIRTY (BAD) then we started new business with PAPPU of ONIONS, we required same energy to peel the ONIONS.

FUNCTIONAL ISOMERISM

Two or more substances with same molecular formula but different functional groups is functional isomerism.

1. Alochol, Ether
2. Alkene, Cycloalkane
3. Cyanide, Isocyanide
4. Aldehyde, Ketone, Oxirane
5. Nitro, Nitrite
6. Acid, Ester, Hydroxyl carbonyl compound (Aldehyde, Ketone)
7. Alkdiene, Alkyne, Cycloalkane

In order to memorise the functional isomerism we need to make relation between them. If you make a story that has a personal meaning, you are more likely to remember it.

1. Alcohol and Ether

Word	PMS
Alcohol	Alcohol bottle
Ether	Thar desert

Visualisation: I am very sad, that is why I am drinking two BOTTLES of ALCOHOL sitting on the sand in THAR DESERT.

2. Acid, ester and Hydroxyl carbonyl Compound (Aldehyde, Ketone)

Word	PMS
Acid	A.C
Ester	Easter festival
Hydroxyl	High drugs
Carbonyl	Car + Boni (a female)

Visulisation: I am taking HIGH DRUGS sitting in a CAR, with BONI, then I switch on the A.C, and we both are celebrating EASTER FESTIVAL in the car only.

3. Alkene and Cycloalkane

Word	PMS
Alkene	Key
Cyclo	Cycle
Alkane	Alka (a beautiful girl)

Visualisation: Lots of KEYS are hanging on the CYCLE of ALKA, (a beautiful girl).

4. Cyanide and Isocyanide

Word	PMS
Cyanide	Cyanide – poison
Isocyanide	Ice for cyanide

Visualisation: I fell down as I smelt CYANIDE, then my friends fed me lots of ICE to nullify the effect of the CYANIDE.

5. Aldehyde, Ketone and Oxirane

Word	PMS
Aldehyde	All + hide
Ketone	Kite
Oxirane	Oxi (female of ox) + rain

Visualisation:
ALL HIDE themselves as they are playing hide and seek.

FAST AND SLOW REACTION

Fast reaction – Activation energy is low.

Slow reaction – Activation energy is high.

Fast reaction: Activation energy is low.

Word	PMS
Activation	Ek (one) + tea + vat

Visualisation: While drinking EK (one) TEA I heard a news that VAT (charges) became LOW. So I sold all things very very FAST.

Slow reaction: Activation energy is high.

Word	PMS
Activation	Ek + tea + vat

Visualisation: while Drinking EK (one) TEA I heard the news that VAT became very HIGH, so customers came very very SLOWLY to purchase the things.

NOTE: In these stories we used the PMS of activation. We didn't use the PMS of energy and reaction. Because students of science already know activation energy is of fast and slow reaction.

DISTINCTION BETWEEN PRIMARY, SECONDARY, TERITIARY ALOCOHOLS

A. LUCAS TEST:

1. If cloudiness appears immediately, tertiary alcohol is indicated.

3. If cloudiness appear only upon heating, primary alcohol is indicated.

Let's learn how to apply creativity and imagination to memorise this.

1. If cloudiness appears immediately, tertiary alcohol is indicated.

Word	PMS
Tertiary	Tertian malaria
Lucas	Luca

Visualisation: Due to drinking of ALCOHOL, I began to suffer from TERTIAN MALARIA, then LUCA carried me IMMEDIATELY on the CLOUD for treatment.

Word	PMS
Secondary	Sicander
Lucas	Luca
5	Five

Visualisation: LUCA and SICANDER are drinking ALCOHOL and in the state of Nasha (hindi word meaning state of intoxication) started cutting CLOUD with KNIFE.

3. If cloudiness appears only upon heating, primary alcohol is indicated.

Word	PMS
Primary	Primary class
Lucas	Luca

Visualisation: LUCA is teaching children of PRIMARY CLASSES in the CLOUD. Due to feeling cold in cloud, he drinks ALCOHOL to HEAT his body.

B. VICTOR MEYER'S TEST

1. If blood red colour appears, it indicates a primary alcohol.
2. If blue colour appears, it indicates a secondary alcohol.

Comprehensive Memory Development Course

3. If colourless, it indicates a tertiary alcohol.

Let's learn how to apply creativity and imagination to memorise these:

1. If blood red colour appears, it indicates a primary alcohol.

Word	PMS
Primary	Primary class
Meyer	Mayor

Visualisation: After VICTORY, MAYOR drinks ALCOHOL sitting in PRIMARY CLASS. The children in the class felt very bad and beat him with stick and rod. Then RED COLOUR BLOOD started coming out from his body.

2. If blue colour appears, it indicates a secondary alcohol.

Word	PMS
Secondary	Sicander
Meyer	Mayor

Visualisation: After VICTORY, SICANDER and MAYOR went to see the movie "BLUE", in which a hero was drinking alcohol. So to follow the hero, they also drank ALCOHOL and enjoyed that movement.

3. If colourless, it indicates a tertiary alcohol.

Word	PMS
Tertiary	Tertian malaria
Meyer	Mayor

Visualisation: After VICTORY, MAYOR drank contaminated ALCOHOL so he started suffering from TERTIAN MALERIA.

THE RELATIVE CONCENTRATION OF H_3O^+ ION AND OH^- ION VARY IN DIFFERENT SOLUTION

1. In neutral solution $[H_3O^+] = [OH^-]$
2. In acidic solution $[H_3O] > [OH^-]$
3. In basic solution $[H_3O] < [OH^-]$

In this example, we will learn how to apply creativity and imagination to memorise this.

1. In neutral solution $[H_3O] = [OH^-]$

Word	PMS
Neutral	New + trolly
H_3O (hydronium ion)	Hydra + onion
OH^- (alcohol)	Hole

Here (=) take as a path on which we walk or we go.

Visualisation: HYDRA collects ONIONS from the PATH, put them in the NEW TROLLY and go inside the HOLE.

2. In acidic solution $[H_3O^+] > [OH^-]$

Word	PMS
H_3O (Hydronium ion)	Hydra + onion
OH (Alcohol)	Hole
Acid (A.C)	A.C
>	Big

Visualisation: BIG HYDRA was harvesting BIG ONION. So he got tired and sat for some time in A.C and again tried to put BIG ONION into a HOLE, but he could not do that because the HOLE was SMALL.

3. In basic solution $[H_3O^+] < [OH^-]$

Word	PMS
Basic	Boss
H_3O^+ (Hydronium ion)	Hydra + onion
OH (Alcohol)	Hole

Visualisation: BOSS is angry with HYDRA. So he throws ONION at him, then Hydra hides himself inside a BIG HOLE where nobody can search him.

DIFFERENCE BETWEEN OXIDATION AND REDUCTION

OXIDATION	REDUCTION
It is the process which involves:	It is the process which involves:
1. Addition of oxygen	1. Removal of oxygen
2. Removal of hydrogen	2. Addition of hydrogen
3. Addition of an electronegative element	3. Removal of an electronegative element
4. Removal of an electropositive element	4. Addition of an electropositive element
5. Loss of an electron	5. Gain of electron

Here we notice that oxidation and reduction are just opposite to each other. If we learn the properties of one, then it would be easy to remember the properties of the other.

WORD	PMS
Reduction	Red + colour duck
Hydrogen	Hydrogen balloon
Oxygen	Ox
Electropositive (+)	Electron + doctor
Electronegativity (-)	Electron + villain

Visualisation: A RED COLOUR DUCK is sitting inside a big HYDROGEN BALLOON. The ox gets injured then DOCTOR OF ELECTRON comes in. First he kills the VILLAIN who has stolen ELECTRON, after that the RED COLOUR DUCK and DOCTOR OF ELECTRON both dance in the HYDROGEN BALLOON. The RED COLOUR DUCK is very fond of ELECTRON and after dancing she takes lots of ELECTRONS and eats all ELECTRONS.

The State of a Variable can be Changed Via a Thermodynamic Process

1. Adiabatic process; $dQ = 0$
2. Isothermal process; $dT = 0$
3. Isobaric process; $dP = 0$
4. Isochoric process; $dV = 0$
5. Cyclic process; $dE = 0$, $dH = 0$

In order to memorise these, we make some funny association which will help these to register in our memory

1. Adiabatic process: $dQ = 0$

WORD	PMS
Adiabatic	Idea sim + bat
dQ	Small queen
0	Hero

Visualisation: The SMALL QUEEN is giving an IDEA SIM to the HERO but he breaks it with a BAT.

2. Isothermal process: $dT=0$

WORD	PMS
Isothermal	Ice + thermacol
dT	Small temple
0	Hero

Visualisation: The SMALL TEMPLE is made up of ICE and starts melting. So the HERO is saving it by wrapping the small temple in a box made with THERMACOL.

3. Isobaric process: $dP=0$

WORD	PMS
Isobaric	Ice + bar
dP	Small parrot
0	Hero

Visualisation: In a BAR, the HERO catches SMALL PARROT and dips it into ICE.

4. Isochoric process: $dV=0$

WORD	PMS
Isochoric	Ice + chor (thief)
dV	Small van
0	Hero

Visualisation: A CHOR (thief) steals the SMALL VAN of the HERO and hides it inside the pile of ICE.

5. Cyclic process: dE and dV=0

WORD	PMS
Cyclic	Cycle
dE	Small elephant
dV	Small van
0	Hero

Visualisation: In a SMALL HOUSE, a competition is going on between a SMALL ELEPHANT

The Criterion of Spontaneity can be Summed as Follows:

Let's learn this by making interesting stories.

WORD	PMS
	Small
G	Goat
Negative	Villain
Spontaneous	Spoon

Visualisation: My SMALL GOAT has become a VILLAIN, she has broken all SPOONS.

WORD	PMS
	Small
G	Goat
0	Hero
Equilibrium	

Visualisation: My SMALL GOAT is a HERO, he is playing a role of EK KULI in a movie.

Comprehensive Memory Development Course

WORD	PMS
	Small
G	Goat
+	Doctor
Non – spontaneous	without spoon

Visualisation: My SMALL GOAT went to a DOCTOR, he suggests that take your meal WITHOUT SPOON.

1. **Protophilic solvent:** solvent with a high tendency to accept proton.
2. **Photogenic solvent:** solvent with a tendency to produce (give) proton.
3. **Amphiprotic solvent:** solvent with a tendency to accept as well as to donate proton.
4. **Aprotic solvent:** Solvent which neither donates nor accepts proton.

In order to memorise this, we need to make a relation between them forming a story to place them permanently in our memory bank.

1. **Protophilic Solvent:** solvent with a high tendency to accept proton.

WORD	PMS
Protophilic	
Solvent	Servant

Visualisation: My SERVANT collects PROTONS and he likes making a FILE of PROTONS.

2. **Protogenic Solvent:** solvent with a tendency to produce proton.

WORD	PMS
Protogenic	Proton + Geni (a girl)
Solvent	Servant

Visualisation: GENI is giving PROTON to the SERVANT.

3. **Amphiprotic Solvent:** solvent with a tendency to accept as well as to donate proton.

WORD	PMS
Amphiprotic	Amphibia (a boy) + proton
Solvent	Servant

Visualisation: AMPHIBIA ate all PROTONS. So my SERVANT beat him with a stick, then AMPHIBIA vomits all PROTONS.

4. **Aprotic Solvent:** Solvent which neither donate nor accept proton.

WORD	PMS
Aprotic	Without proton
Solvent	Servant

Visualisation: My SERVANT lives WITHOUT PROTON, he neither takes PROTON from others nor gives PROTON to anyone.

What is Carbon dating? How is this process used in the determination of the age of archaeological artefacts?

1. Carbon dating is a method of determining the age of fossils, dead plants from the proportion of Carbon-14 (C14) relative to Carbon-12 (C12)
2. Carbon-14 is a radioisotope formed by bombardment of nitrogen-14.
3. Plants and animals absorb C14 from the atmosphere.
4. When plants and animals die, they stop taking in C14 and the trapped C14 in them decays into nitrogen by emitting Beta particles.
5. In 5600 years, half the amount of C14 decays into nitrogen.

the time elapsed since the death of the organism. This technique of estimating the time interval is known as Carbon Dating.

PMS:

We will learn this with the help of cartoons instanty.

1. Dating — Age – Proportion of C14 to C12

2. C14 is a Radio (jockey) in a station called Isotope Bombardment of Nitrogen 14.

3.  Plants and Animals absorb C14 (as so cute).

4.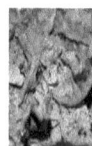

     DIE   Stopped   trapped   decay

5.

the time elapsed since the death of the organism.

INTENSIVE PROPERTY AND EXTENSIVE PROPERTY

Intensive property: The properties which do not depend upon the quantity of matter, pressure,

Extensive property: The properties which depend upon the quantity of matter volume, number of moles, enthalpy, entropy, mass, energy and heat capacity.

In order to memorise these triad groups, we would make some funny associations.

Intensive property: The properties which do not depend upon the quantity of matter, pressure,

WORD	PMS
Density	Den + city
Concentration	Ocean
Refractive	Refree
Index	Index
Viscosity	Whisky
	Space + heat

Visualisation: In OCEAN, I live in big SPACE because I produce HEAT. One day I went to the DEN of the CITY where in a TENIS game, the REFREE was in PRESSURE because his team was losing, he sat on DESK; his TEMPERATURE became high so he drank VISKY (WHISKY).

Extensive property: The property which depends upon the quantity of matter, volume, number of moles, enthalpy, entropy, mass, energy and heat capacity.

WORD	PMS
Extensive	Axe + tenis
Heat capacity	Heat + cap + city
Enthalpy	Therapy
Entropy	Trophy

Visualisation: Taking an AXE I went to see a TENIS match where only those people were allowed who have QUANTITY. I sat and shouted with high VOLUME. I felt some fault in my MASS (muscles), then I applied a THERAPY. I got ENERGY from HEAT, after that I took a CAP from the CITY, where a NUMBER OF MALLS were opened. Those who purchase from there, got TROPHY.

BUFFER SOLUTION

The solution which maintains its pH constant even upon the addition of small amount of acid or base is called a buffer solution.

WORD	PMS
PH	pitch
Base	boss
Buffer	buffer system

Visualisation: I am making a SOLUTION in which I am adding small amount of ACIDS and give it to BOSS to maintain the concentration on PITCH in which BUFFER SYSTEM is going.

Buffer solutions are of two types:

1. **Acidic buffer:** A buffer solution with pH less than 7 is called acidic buffer.

$$pH = pK_a + \log \frac{[Salt]}{[Acid]}$$

2. **Basic buffer:** A buffer solution with pH more than 7 is called basic buffer.

$$pOH = pK_b + \log \frac{[Salt]}{[Acid]}$$

In order to memorise these, we should make some funny associations to give them a permanent space in our memory.

1. **Acidic buffer:** A buffer solution with pH less than 7 is called acidic buffer.

WORD	PMS
Buffer	Buffer system
pH	Pitch
7	Heaven

Visualisation: I am organising a BUFFER SOLUTION on the PITCH which is situated in a height LESS than HEAVEN.

Acidic buffer – $pH = pK_a + \log \dfrac{[Salt]}{[Acid]}$

WORD	PMS
pH	Pitch
pK_a	(true)

Comprehensive Memory Development Course

+	Doctor
Log	(people)
Salt	Salty mixer
Acid	A.c

Visualisation: I am walking on the PITCH; my PAKKA friend is coming towards me with a DOCTOR and with many LOG (people) for walking because they are suffering from illnesss. They drank SALTY mixture after they sat in A.C, so they became ill.

Basic buffer: A buffer solution having P^H more than 7 is called basic buffer.

WORD	PMS
Basic	Boss
Buffer	Buffer system
pH	Pitch
7	Heaven

Visualisation: My BOSS became angry so he decided to make a PITCH biggar than HEAVEN to organise a big BUFFER SYSTEM.

Basic buffer – $pOH = pKb + \log \dfrac{[Salt]}{[Acid]}$

WORD	PMS
P	Parrots
K	KBR
+	Doctor
Log	(people)
Base	Boss
OH	Hole
Salt	Salty mixture

Visualisation: Lots of PARROTS are sitting in the HOLE, they heard some noise, so they go towards another PARROT who fall down in KBR. A DOCTOR comes and orders LOG (people) To make SALT and he chided the BOSS. It heapened because of him.

pH=14 - pOH

WORD	PMS
pH	Pitch
14	Chair

P	Parrot
-	Bad
OH	Hole

Visualisation: In the PITCH, a CHAIR has been kept. A bad PARROT is making a HOLE in it.

IMPORTANT TERMS AND COMMON NAMES

1. Sand is silicon dioxide – SiO_2
2. Washing soda is Na_2CO_3
3. Water glass is sodium silicate – Na_2SiO_3
4. Dry ice – CO_2
5. Caro's acid – H_2SO_5

We can memorise these important terms and common name by fabricating a funny and interesting story and by joining all the word together.

1. Sand is silicon dioxide – $SiO2$

WORD	PMS
Sand	Sunday
Si (silicon)	Sita
O_2	Oat

Visualisation: SITA MAA is watching the SUNDAY movie and eating OAT.

2. Washing soda is Na_2CO_3

WORD	PMS
Washing	Washing machine
Soda	Soda
Na_2	Nattu (a boy)
CO_3	Coti (small coat)

Visualisation: The WASHING MACHINE is full of SODA. NATTU (a boy) pores his COTI and starts washing.

3. Water glass is sodium silicate – Na_2SiO_3

WORD	PMS
Na_2	Nattu (a boy)
Si	Sita Maa
O	Ox
3	Tree

Visualisation: NATTU give a GLASS of WATER to SITA MAA who is sitting on the OX under the TREE.

4. Dry ice – CO_2

WORD	PMS
C	Car
O	OX
2	SHOES

Visualisation: I hit my CAR to an OX, he picks my DRY SHOES and washes with ICE to make cool-cool.

5. Caro's acid – H_2SO_5

WORD	PMS
Caro	Crorepati (millionaire)
H_2	Hut
S	Sulpha
O	Ox
5	Knife

Visualisation: CROREPATI (millionaire) people burn the HUTS of poor people and enjoy smoking SULPHA then an OX becomes angry; he throws ACID to all CROREPATI and kills them with a KNIFE.

SOME IMPORTANT TERMS

Terms   Characteristics

(Z=Atomic No, A=Mass No, N=Neutron, P=Proton)

1. Isotopes : Z= Same, A = Different
2. Isobars : Z = Different, A= Same
3. Isotones : N = Same, Nucleous – Different

In order to memorise this we need to make a connection between them.

1. Isotopes   Z=same; A=different

WORD	PMS
Isotopes	Ice + topes
Z	Zebra
A	Aeroplane

Visualisation: At the TOPES of ICE, a ZEBRA is cleaning an AEROPLANE boarding different people.

2. Isobars   Z=different; A=same

WORD	PMS
Isobar	Ice+bar
Z	Zebra
A	Apple

Visualisation: A BEAR of ICE eats an APPLE and goes to visit different ZOO.

3. Isotones   N=same; Nucleons=different

WORD	PMS
Isotones	Ice + tonic
N	Nuns
Nucleons	New + lion

Visualisation: NUNS mix ICE in TONIC and gives NEW different-different LIONS.

NOTES: Students of Science know very well about this. (Z=Atomic No, A=Mass No, N=Neutron, P=Proton). Here we are taking only the code.

DIFFERENCE BETWEEN ALKANE, ALKENE AND ALKYNE

ALKANE

General formula	C_nH_2n+2
C—C Bond length	$1.54A^0$
C—H Bond length	$1.12A^0$
Shape	Tetrahedral
Bond angle	109.5'
Hybridisation	SP^3
Alkane is also called	

Let us make a connection between them.

General formula	C_nH_2n+2
WORD	**PMS**
Alkane	Alka (a lady)
+	Doctor
2	Zoo

Visualisation: ALKA is walking with a DOCTOR in a ZOO.

C—C Bond length 1.54A^0

WORD	PMS
Alkane	Alka
C—C	Sisi (in pronounce)
Bond length (B.L)	Bill
1	Raja (king)
.	Spot
54 (L,r)	Lawyer

Visualisation: ALKA took SISI without paying BILL, so RAJA (king) with SPOTTED face complained her to LAWER.

C—H Bond length 1.12A^0

WORD	PMS
Carbon(C)	Car
Hydrogen	Hydrogen balloon
Alkane	Alka
Bond length (B.L)	Bill
1	Raja
.	Spot
12 (d,n)	Den

Visualisation: ALKA hits CAR on a big HYDROGEN BALLOON, so she had to pay BILL for it, she and RAJA, SITTING in SPOTTED CAR they went to DEN.

Shape   Tetrahedral

WORD	PMS
Alkane	Alka
Tetrahedral	Tractor + hydra

Visualisation: ALKA and HYDRA are giving SHAPE to TRACTOR.

Bond angle   109.5'

WORD	PMS
Alkane	Alka
Bond angle (B.A)	B.A degree
109 (d.s.p)	D.S.P
.	Spoted
5	Wife
'	Degree

Visualisation: ALKA is a B.A pass student, she became D.S.P. She caught and punished SPOTTED wife in a MINUTE.

Hybridisation   SP^3

WORD	PMS
Hybridisation	High + bridge
Sp	S.P
3	Three monkey of Gandhiji
Alkane	Alka

Visualisation: ALKA is S.P. She is catching THREE MONKEYS OF GANDHIJI, they are Sitting on the HIGH BRIDGE.

WORD	PMS
Alkane	Alka
	Per (foot) + fain (froth)

Visualisation: ALKA washing his PER with FAIN.

ALKENE

General formula	CnH2n
C=C Bond length	1.34A^0
C—H Bond length	1.10A^0
Bond angle	120^0
Hybridisation	SP^2
Shape	Trigonal planner
Alkene is called	

Let us make a connection between them.

C=C Bond length   1.34A0

WORD	PMS
Alkene	Key
C=C	Sisi (bottle)
Bond length (B.L)	Bill
1	Raja (king)
34 (m,r)	Mare (female horse)
= (double bond)	Double roti

Visualisation: RAJA feds DOUBLE ROTI to MARE and rode on it. He hit that SISI With the KEY and he didn't pay BILL.

C—H Bond length $1.10A^0$

WORD	PMS
Carbon(C)	Car
Hydrogen	Hydrogen balloon
Alkene	Key
Bond length (B.L)	Bill
1	Raja
.	Spot
10	Hen

Visualisation: I opened my CAR with a KEY and started driving. Suddenly from a big HYDROGEN BALLOON, RAJA comes and gives SPOTTED HENS as a gift but he also shows me the BILL of the gift.

Bond angle   120°

WORD	PMS
Bond angle (B.A)	B.A degree
Alkene	Key
120 (t,n,s)	Tennis

Visualisation: I am B.A pass; I have the KEY of success in TENNIS.

Hybridisation   SP²

WORD	PMS
Hybridisation	High + bridge
Sp	S.P
2	Zoo

Visualisation: S.P opens HIGH BRIDGE with KEY which has big ZOO inside it.

Shape   Trigonal planner

WORD	PMS
Alkene	Key
Trigonal	Trokon (triangle)
Planer	Plane

Visualisation:

WORD	PMS
Alkene	Key
	Oil + fain

Visualisation: I am rubbing OIL on my KEYS and wash it with FAINS .

ALKYNE

General formula	CnH_2n-_2
C C Bond length	$1.20A^0$
C—H Bond length	$1.08A^0$
Bond angle	180^0
Hybridisation	SP
Shape	Linear

Let us make a connection between them.

General formula	CnH_2n-2	
WORD	**PMS**	
Alkyne	Kye (greenish black muddy water or algae)	
—	Villain	
2	Shoes	

Visualisation: VILLAIN beat me with SHOES and throws me inside KYE (algae).

NOTE: CnH2n is common in alkane, alkene, alkyne

C C Bond length	$1.20A^0$
Alkyne	Key
C C	Sisi (in pronounce)
Bond length (B.L)	Bill
1	Raja
.	Spot
20 (n,s)	Nose

Visualisation: I collected KYE in SISI but I didn't pay BILL, when I go in front of RAJA he made SPOT on my NOSE.

C—H Bond length   1.08A

WORD	PMS
Carbon(C)	Car
Hydrogen	Hydrogen balloon
Alkene	Key
Bond length (B.L)	Bill
1	Raja
.	Spot
08 (s,f)	Sofa

Visualisation: I hit CAR on HYDROGEN BALLOON, so it got damaged, I had to pay BILL, I went inside it, I saw RAJA is sitting on SPOTTED SOFA.

Bond angle   **180°**

WORD	PMS
Bond angle (B.A)	B.A degree
Alkyne	Kye (Green Thing in water)
180 (d,v,s)	Dove soap

Visualisation: I am B.A pass but still I didn't get success, so I tore my B.A DEGREE in KYE (Greenish things in water), I felt good by washing it with DOVE SOAP.

Hybridisation   **SP**

WORD	PMS
Hybridisation	High + bridge
Sp	S.P
Alkyne	Kye

Visualisation: S.P ordered to built HIGH BRIDGE over KYES.

Shape   **Linear**

WORD	PMS
Alkyne	Kye
Linear	Line

Visualisation: LINE by LINE we are SHAPE of KYES.

COMPARISON OF WHITE AND RED PHOSPHORUS

Coding in visual images is particularly useful in memorising the comparison of white and red phosphorus as well. We can arrange the terms in story to get some visual image.

Properties	White Phosphorus
Colour	white
Smell	garlic like
	1.83 – 1.85
Physiological effect	poisonous
m.p/^{0}c	44
ionisation temperature	30
with cl$_2$	React at room temperature
Action of air	Phosphorescence
with NaoH	PH$_3$ is formed
state	Waxy solid, can be cut with knife

Let's make code and an interesting story.

WORD	PMS
Gravity	Grave
NaoH	Soap
1	Sun
83 (f,m)	Foam
85 (f,l)	(fruits)
Melting point (m.p)	M.P (state)
44 (r,r)	River
30 (m,z)	Moza
Cl (chlorine)	Clown
Phosphorus	Fox with pores

Visualisation: A WHITE COLOUR FOX WITH PORES was SMELLING like GARLIC, In the SPACE, she was sitting on the GRAVE, seeing the SUN (1) there was a big FOAM (83) on which FALS (fruits) (85) was putting. She tested but their test was POISONOUS, then she went to M.P by swimming in the RIVER (44) so she started suffering from COLD. To IGNITE (warm) her body she wore MOZA (30). A CLOWN proposed her to dance at ROOM, suddenly the AIR started blowing. Then she appeared like PHOSPHORESCENCE. During dance she slipped on the SOAP but FOX was FINE, she cut the SOLID WAX with KNIFE and ate to get relief.

PROPERTIES	RED PHOSPHORUS
Colour	Reddish – violet
Space gravity	2.06 – 2.39
m.p/^{0}c	600

igniting temperature	260
with clown	Read only when heated
state	brittle powder

WORD	PMS
Space gravity	Space + grave
Melting point (m.p)	M.P (state)
Phosphorus	Fox with pores
2	Zoo
06 (s,ch)	Sachin tendulkar
39 (m,b)	Mobile
600 (gss)	Gasses
260 (ngs)	Nags
Chlorine	Clown

Visualisation: A RED COLOUR FOX WITH PORES was eating RADDISH, wearing VIOLET COLOUR dress. In the SPACE there was a big GRAVE in the ZOO (2). Sitting on it, she talked with SACHIN TENDULKAR on MOBILE (39) that in the M.P, GASSES were blowing, due to IGNITION all NAGS (260) were dying. A CLOWN is very hungry; he heated them and ate them by BRITTLE POWDER.

PREPARATIONS OF COMPOUNDS

1. Preparation of chloroform

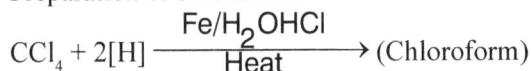

$$CCl_4 + 2[H] \xrightarrow[\text{Heat}]{\text{Fe/H}_2\text{OHCl}} \text{(Chloroform)}$$

2. Preparation of chloropicrin

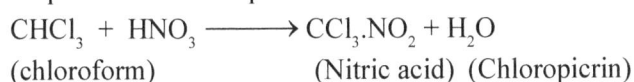

$$CHCl_3 + HNO_3 \longrightarrow CCl_3.NO_2 + H_2O$$
(chloroform)   (Nitric acid) (Chloropicrin)

3. Preparation of methane

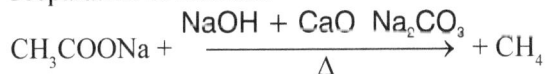

$$CH_3COONa + \xrightarrow[\Delta]{\text{NaOH + CaO Na}_2\text{CO}_3} + CH_4$$

4. Preparation of phosgene

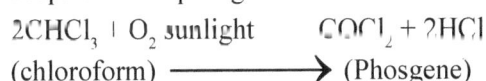

$$2CHCl_3 + O_2 \text{ sunlight} \quad COCl_2 + 2HCl$$
(chloroform) $\longrightarrow$ (Phosgene)

5. Preparation of carbonic acid

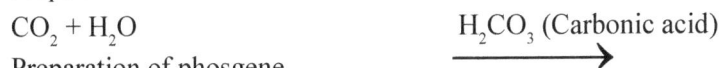

$$CO_2 + H_2O \xrightarrow{\hspace{3cm}} H_2CO_3 \text{ (Carbonic acid)}$$

6. Preparation of phosgene

$$CCl_4 + H_2O \xrightarrow{\hspace{3cm}} COCl_2 + 2HCl$$
(Phosgene)

7. Preparation of producer gas

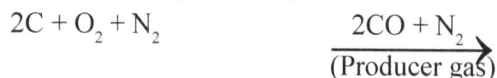

$$2C + O_2 + N_2 \xrightarrow{\quad} \underset{\text{(Producer gas)}}{2CO + N_2}$$

8. Preparation of aldehyde

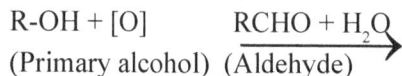

$$\underset{\text{(Primary alcohol)}}{R\text{-}OH + [O]} \xrightarrow{\quad} \underset{\text{(Aldehyde)}}{RCHO + H_2O}$$

9. Preparation of methane

$$\underset{\text{(Chloroform)}}{CHCl_3\ Zn + H_2O} \xrightarrow{\quad} \underset{\text{(Methane)}}{CH_4 + 3HCl}$$

10. Preparation of sodium sulphate

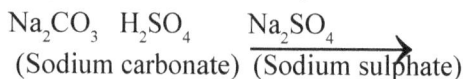

$$\underset{\text{(Sodium carbonate)}}{Na_2CO_3\ H_2SO_4} \xrightarrow{\quad} \underset{\text{(Sodium sulphate)}}{Na_2SO_4}$$

In order to memorise the preparation of compounds, we need to make relation between them.

1. Preparation of chloroform

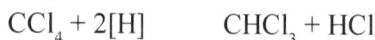

$$CCl_4 + 2[H] \xrightarrow{\quad} CHCl_3 + HCl$$

WORD	PMS
Carbon (C)	Car
Chlorine (Cl)	Clown
Hydrogen (H)	Hydrogen balloon
Iron (Fe)	Iron
$CHCl_3$	Chloroform
HCl	Hackle

Visualisation: A CLOWN parks the CAR at the DOOR of the ZOO, then he goes inside a big HYDROGEN balloon which is made of IRON, he washes it with WATER and to initiate he gives HEAT, suddenly I come there, I made him to CHLOROFORM and killed him with HACKLE.

2. Preparation of chloropicrin

$$CHCl_3 + HNO_3 \xrightarrow{\quad} CCl_3.NO_2 + H_2O$$

WORD	PMS
$CHCl_3$	Chloroform
Nitric acid	Nai (barber) + trick
Chloropicrin	Clown + pic + rin soap

Visualisation: A Nai is playing a TRICK to make CLOWN smell CHLOROFORM, who is PICKING RIN SOAP from WATER.

3. Preparation of methane

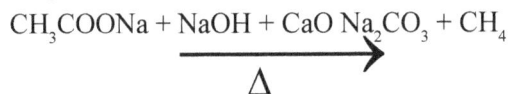

$$CH_3COONa + NaOH + CaO \xrightarrow{\Delta} Na_2CO_3 + CH_4$$

WORD	PMS
Sodium acitate	Soda + bottle + state
Sodalime	Sodalime
Na2	Natu (my friend)
CO3	Carbonate
Methane	Mithun (actor)
	Heat

Visualisation: I sell SODA BOTTLE in all STATE. I prepare it by mixing SODA with LIME, after that I HEAT it. My friend NATU steals it and hide inside the CARBONNATE, little bit he drinks and starts dancing with MITHUN.

4. Preparation of phosgene

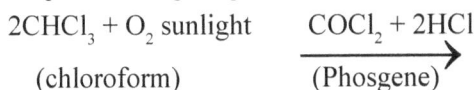

$$2CHCl_3 + O_2 \text{ sunlight} \xrightarrow{} COCl_2 + 2HCl$$
$$\text{(chloroform)} \qquad \text{(Phosgene)}$$

WORD	PMS
$CHCl_3$	Chloroform
O_2	Oat (in pronounce)
Phosgene	Fox + gene
HCl	Hackle

Visualisation: I ate OAT full of CHLOROFORM, sitting under the SUNLIGHT, I became ill. Then a FOX is wearing GENES came to me and started combing my hair with HACKLE.

5. Preparation of carbonic acid

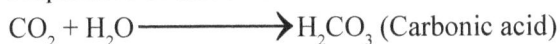

$$CO_2 + H_2O \xrightarrow{} H_2CO_3 \text{ (Carbonic acid)}$$

WORD	PMS
CO_2	Coat (in pronounce)
Carbonic acid	Car + Boni Kapoor + Acid

Visualisation: I wash my COAT with WATER, I hang it on the CAR, then BONI KAPOOR throws ACID on it to damage.

6. Preparation of phosgene

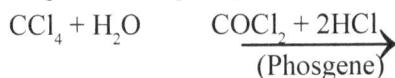

$$CCl_4 + H_2O \xrightarrow{} COCl_2 + 2HCl$$
$$\text{(Phosgene)}$$

239

WORD	PMS
Carbon (C)	Car
Chlorine (Cl)	Clown
Phosgene	Fox + gene
4	*Chor* (thief)
HCl	Hackle

Visualisation: A CLOWN is washing the CAR at the DOOR with WATER. A FOX wearing GENES gives a HACKLE for his work.

7. Preparation of producer gas

$$2C + O_2 + N_2 \qquad 2CO + N_2$$
$$\xrightarrow{\text{(Producer gas)}}$$

WORD	SUBATITUTE
Carbon(C)	Car
O_2	Oat
Nitrogen (N)	Nitrogen
2	Couple
Producer gas	Producer

Visualisation: At NIGHT, COUPLES are eating OAT sitting in a CAR. The PRODUCER gave this scene to play.

8. Preparation of aldehyde

$$R\text{-}OH + [O] \longrightarrow RCHO + H_2O$$
(Primary alcohol)   (Aldehyde)

WORD	PMS
Primary alcohol	Primary class + Alcohol
Oxygen (O)	Ox
Aldehyde	All + hide

Visualisation: The OXES are sitting in PRIMARY CLASS, drinking ALCOHOL, after Drinking ALL HIDE inside the WATER.

9. Preparation of methane

$$CHCl_3 \ Zn + H_2O \longrightarrow CH_4 + 3HCl$$
(Chloroform)   (Methane)

WORD	PMS
Methane	Mithun
Zinc (Zn)	Zin
HCl	Hackle

Comprehensive Memory Development Course

Visualisation: A ZIN (Genni) smells CHLOROFORM and falls down into the WATER. Then MITHUN picks him up with the help of HACKLE.

10. Preparation of sodium sulphate

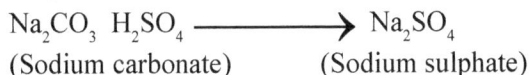

$$Na_2CO_3 \ H_2SO_4 \longrightarrow Na_2SO_4$$
(Sodium carbonate)　　　(Sodium sulphate)

WORD	PMS
Na_2	Natu (in pronounce)
CO_3	Car bonnet
SO_4	Safar (journey)
Sulfuric acid	Sulpha + rick

Visualisation: NATU is tighting the CAR BONNET, smoking SULPHA. After some time he throw SULPHA on RICK. After that NATU get ready to go for SAFAR (journey).

IMPORTANT ALLOYS

1. LA 141 $Mg + Al + Li$
2. Alpax $Si + Al$
3. Perm alloy $Fe + Ni + C$
4. Bearing metal $Cu + Zn +$
5. Hydrone $Na + Pb$
6. Ferrosilicon $Fe + S$
7. Bross $Cu + Zn$
8. Coin alloy (white) $Cu + Ag + Zn + Ni$
9. Coin alloy (red) $Cu + Zn + Sn$
10. Britannia metal $Sn + Sb + Cu + Zn$
11. Broze $Cu + Sn$
12. German silver $Zn + Ni + Cu$
13. Dutch metal $Cu + Zn$
14. Constantan $Cu + Ni$
15. Newton metal $Sn + Pb$
16. Nickeloy $Ni + Cu + Al$
17. Bell metal $Cu + Sn$
18. Type metal $Pb + Sb + Sn$
19. Alnico $Al + Ni + Co + Fe + Cu$
20. Manganium $Ni + Cu + Mn$
21. Devarda's alloy $Cu + Zn + Al$
22. Gunmetal $Cu + Sn + Zn$

23.	Cunico	$Cu + Co + Fe + Ni$
24.	Monel metal	$Cu + Mn + Fe + Ni$
25.	Pewter	$Pb + Sn$
26.	Nickel steel	$Fe + Ni$
27.	Rose metal	$Bi + Pb + Zn + Cd$
28.	Electron	$Mg + Zn$
29.	Nimonic series	$Ti + Ni + Co + Al + Cr$
30.	White metal	$Sb + Cu + Sn$
31.	Stainless steel	$Fe + Ni + Cr + C$
32.	Magnalium	$Al + Mg$
33.	Invar	$Fe + Ni$
34.	Aluminium bronze	$Cu + Al$
35.	Amalgam	Metal coated with Hg
36.	Solder	$Pb + Sn$
37.	Babbit metal	$Cu + Sn + Sb$
38.	Delta metal	$Cu + Zn + Fe$
39.	Duralumin	$Zn + Cu + Mg + Al$
40.	Wood's metal	$Sn + Bi + Pb + Cd$
41.	Rolled gold	$Cu + Al$
42.	Platinate	$Fe + Ni$
43.	Phosphor bronze	$Cu + Sn + P$
44.	Ferrochrome	$Fe + Cr$
45.	Ferromanganese	$Fe + Mn$
46.	– alloy	$Al + Cu + Mg + Ni$
47.	Nichrome	$Fe + Ni + Mn + Cr$
48.	Hostelloy c nichrome	$Ni + Cr$
49.	Manganese steel	$Fe + Mn + C$

In order to memorise important alloys, we need to make connections between them.

1. L A 141 $Mg + Al + Li$

Word	PMS
LA	LA (passage between mountains)
141	ToRToise (141)
Al + mg	All Maggie (entire magggie noodles)
Li	Lichee (a juicy fruit)

Visualisation: A tortoise was sitting in the LA and ate all maggie and Liches.

Comprehensive Memory Development Course

2. Alpax Si + Al

Word	PMS
Alpax	Alp (mountain peak) + Axe
Si	Sita maa
Al	Alloo (potato)

Visualisation: SITA MAA is sitting at the ALP, she is cutting ALLOO with AXE.

3. Perm alloy Fe + Ni +C

Word	PMS
Perm	Permanently
Fe + Ni	Fenny (daldal)
C	Car

Visualisation: My CAR PERMANENTLY trapped in FENNY.

4. Bearing metal Cu + Zn +Sb

Word	PMS
Bear	Bear (sharab)
Zn	Zin
Cu	Cup
Sb	Aunty

Visualisation: AUNTY is serving BEAR to ZIN in CUP.

5. Hydrone Na + Pb

Word	PMS
Hydrone	High + drone (male of the honey bee)
Na	Soda bottle
Pb	Pub

Visualisation: A HIGH DRONE is very sad. He goes to PUB and drinks SODA to forget his sorrows.

6. Ferrosilion Fe + Si

Word	PMS
Ferrosilicon	Fair + Sita
Fe + Si	Fesial (Facial)

Visualisation: After FACIAL, FAIRNESS appeared on the face of SITA.

7. Brass Cu + Zn

Word	PMS
Brass	Brass utensils
Cu (copper)	Cup
Zn (zinc)	Zin

Visualisation: A ZIN is living in the CUP made up of BRASS.

8. Coin alloy (white) Cu + Ag +Zn +Ni

Word	PMS
Cu (copper)	Cup
Ag (silver)	Silver
Zn + Ni	Zini

Visualisation: A ZIN came out of a WHITE CUP, made up of SILVER. He distributed WHITE COINS to the people wearing WHITE dress.

9. Coin alloy (red)   Cu + Zn + Sn

Word	PMS
Cu + Sn	Cousin
Sn (tin)	Son

Visualisation: A ZIN was counting RED COINS. His COUSIN came and snatched RED COINS from him.

10. Britannia metal   Cu +Sn +Sb +Zn

Word	PMS
Britannia	Britannia biscuit
Cu + Sn	Cousin
Sb (Antimony)	Aunty
Zn (zin)	Zin (magical genni)

Visualisation: ZIN is eating BRITANNIA BISCUITS made of METAL. AUNTY and her COUSIN are begging.

11. Bronze   Cu + Sn

Word	PMS
Bronze	Bronze medal
Cu + Sn	Cousin

Visualisation: My COUSIN got BRONZE MEDAL in games.

12. German silver   Zn + Ni + Cu

Word	PMS
Germal	`Germs
Silver	Silver
Zn + Ni	Zini (female zin)
Cu(copper)	Cup

Visualisation: ZINI (Zn + Ni) is coming out of a CUP (COPPER) made up of SILVER as it contains so many GERMS (GERMAL).

13. Dutch metal   Cu +Zn

Word	PMS
Dutch	Dutch language
Cu (copper)	Cup
Zn (zinc)	Zin

Visualisation: A ZIN (Zn) likes DUTCH LANGUAGE. Person who talks to him in DUTCH LANGUAGE, ZIN (Zn) gives them a CUP (Cu) of METAL.

14. Constantan   Cu +Ni

Word	PMS
Constantan	Constable
Cu (copper)	Cup
Ni (nickel)	Ni

Visualisation: A CONSTABLE is hiding CUP (Cu) inside his KNICKER (Ni).

15. Newton metal   Sn + pb

Word	PMS
Newton	Scientist (Newton)
Sn (Tin)	Son
Pb (Lead)	Pub

Visualisation: SCIENTIST NEWTON was doing practical of METAL. His SON (Sn) comes and asks him to go to PUB.

16. Nickeloy   Ni + Cu + Al

Word	PMS
Nickeloy	Nikhil (A boy)
Cu (copper)	Cup
Al (aluminium)	Alloo
Ni (nickel)	Knicker

Visualisation: A CUP is full of ALLOO. NIKHIL covers it with KNICKER.

17. Bell metal   Cu + Sn

Word	PMS
Bell metal	Bell metal
Cu + Sn	Cousin

Visualisation: My COUSIN (Cu + Sn) is making noise by ringing BELL of METAL.

18. Type metal   Pb + Sb + Sn

Word	PMS
Type metal	typing metal machine

Pb (lead)	Pub
Sb (antimony)	Aunty
Sn (tin)	*Son*

Visualisation: AUNTY and her SON work in a PUB. They prepare bill with the TYPING METAL MACHINE .

19. Alnico   Co + Al + Fe + Ni + Cu

Word	PMS
Alnico	All + nicotine
Co + Al	Coyal
Fe + Ni	Fenny

Visualisation: COYAL brings out a CUP from FENNY and ate ALL NICOTINE.

20. Manganium   Ni + Cu + Mn

Word	PMS
Mn +Ni	Money
Cu (copper)	Cup
Manganium	Meghna

Visualisation: MEGHNA is counting MONEY and pouring it in the CUP.

21. Devendra's alloy   Cu + Zn + Al

Word	PMS
Devard	Devar
Cu (cup)	Cup
Zn (zinc)	Zin
Al (alumin)	Alloo

Visualisation: ZIN gives a CUP to my DEVAR (brother-in-law) and orders him to bring ALLOO.

22. Gun metal   Cu + Sn + Zn

Word	PMS
Gun metal	A gun emitting metal
Cu + Sn	Cushion
Zinc (Zn)	(Ghost)

Visualisation: A ZIN (Zn) is protecting himself from the METAL coming out of a GUN by hiding himself behind a CUSHION (Cu + Sn).

23. Cunico   Co + Cu + Fe + Ni

Word	PMS
Cunico	A cunning man
Cu (Copper)	Cup

Co (Cobalt)	Bolt
Fe + Ni	Fenny

Visualisation: A CUP (Cu) is putting on the FENNY, a CUNNING MAN is breaking it by throwing BOLT.

24. Monel metal   Cu + Mn +Fe + Ni

Word	**PMS**
Monel	Mona
Cu + Mn	Cumin
Fe + Ni	Fenny

Visualisation: MONA (Monel) is growing CUMIN (Cu + Mn) in the FENNY (Fe + Ni) of METAL.

25. Pewter   Pn + sn

Word	**PMS**
Pewter	Potter
Pb (Lead)	Pub
Sn (Tin)	Son

Visualisation: POTTER makes pot and his SON goes to sell in PUB.

26. Nickel steel   Fe + Ni

Word	**PMS**
Nickel	Knicker
Steel	Tea
Fe + Ni	Fenny

Visualisation: You are drinking TEA wearing KNICKER sitting on the FENNY.

27. Rose metal   Bi + Pb + Zn + Cd

Word	**PMS**
Rose metal	Rose of metal
Bi + Pb	Bipasa Basu
Zn (Zin)	
Cd(cadmium)	Candle

Visualisation: A ZIN gives ROSE of METAL to BIPASA BASU and they both go for CANDLE light dinner.

28. Electron   Mg + Zn

Word	**PMS**
Mg (magnesium)	Maggie
Zn (Zinc)	Zin

Visualisation: ELECTRONS are revolving in MAGGIE and ZIN is eating it.

29. Nimonic series   Ti + Ni + Co + Al + Cr

Word	PMS
Nimonic	Pneumonia
Co + Al	Coyal
Ti + Ni	Tiny
Cr (Cromium)	Crow

Visualisation: When I suffered from PNEUMONIA, a TINY COYAL and CROW had taken care of me.

30. White metal   Sb + Cu + Sn

Word	PMS
Sb (antimony)	Aunty
Cu + Sn	Cousin

Visualisation: COUSIN of my AUNTY is very WHITE like METAL.

31. Stainless steel   Fe +Ni + Cr + C

Word	PMS
Fe + Ni	Fenny
Cr (Cromium)	Crow
C (Carbon)	Car

Visualisation: My bright STAINLESS STEEL CAR stucked in FENNY. Then a powerfull CROW pulled it out.

32. Magnalium   Al + Mg

Word	PMS
Magnalium	Meghna (a girl)
Al + Mg	All Maggie

Visualisation: MEGHANA has eaten ALL MAGGIE.

33. Invar   Fe + Ni

Word	PMS
Invar	Inverter
Fe + Ni	Fenny

Visualisation: I charge my INVERTER from FENNY.

34. Aluminium bronze Cu + Al

Word	PMS
Al (Aluminium)	Alloo
Cu (Copper)	Cup

Comprehensive Memory Development Course

Visualisation: A CUP of BRONZE is full of ALLOO.

35. Amalgam   Metal + Hg

Word	PMS
Amalgam	Amul +
Hg (mercury)	Mercury bulb\

Visualisation: I am sitting under the MURCURY BULB, eating AMUL'S JAM.

36. Solder   Pb + Sn

Word	PMS
Solder	Soldier
Pb (Lead)	Pub
Sn (Tin)	Son

Visualisation: Your SON in a PUB is behaving like a brave SOLDIER after drinking.

37. Babbit metal   Cu + Sn + Sb

Word	PMS
Babbit metal	baby mental
Cu + Sn	Cousin
Sb (Antimony)	Aunty

Visualisation: My COUSIN and a mental baby and AUNTY is breaking up Their relation.

38. Delta metal   Cu + Zn + Fe

Word	PMS
Delta	Delta of metal
Cu (Copper)	Cup
Zn (Zinc)	
Fe (Iron)	Iron tablets

Visualisation: A ZIN came out of a CUP. He went to the DELTA of METAL where he ate IRON TEBLETS, and slept.

39. Duraliumin   Zn + Cu + Mg + Al

Word	PMS
Duraliumin	Durable
Mg + Al	Mugal
Zn (Zinc)	Zin
Cu (Copper)	Cup

Visualisation: A ZIN came out from a CUP, he warned the MUGALS that you were not DURABLE to live in India.

40. Wood metal   Sn + Bi + Pb + Cd

Word	PMS
Wood metal	Metal of wood
Sn (Tin)	Son
Bi + Pb	Bipasa Basu
Cd (Cadmium)	Candle

Visualisation:
of a METAL.

41. Rolled gold   Cu + Al

Word	PMS
Cu (Copper)	Cup
Al (Aluminium)	Alloo
Rolled gold	Rolled gold

Visualisation:

42. Palatinate   Fe + Ni

Word	PMS
Palatinate	Plate + net
Fe + Ni	Fenny

Visualisation: I covered PLATE with NET and hide inside the FENNY .

43. Phosphor bronze   Cu + Sn + P

Word	PMS
Phosphor	Fox with pore
Bronze	Bronze clothes
Cu + Sn	Cousin
P (Phosphorus)	Parrot

Visualisation: My COUSIN (Cu + Sn) is hiding a PARROT inside the FOX WITH PORES and covering it with BRONZE CLOTHES.

44. Ferrochrome   Fe + Cr

Word	PMS
Ferrochrome	Fair + crome colour
Fe (Iron)	Iron tablets
Cr (Cromium)	Crow

Visualisation: In the FAIR, CROW buys IRON TABLETS to become of CROME COLOUR.

45. Ferromanganese   Fe + Mn

Word	PMS
Ferromanganese	Mangoes in fair

Fe + Mn	Few man

Visualisation: FEW MAN (Fe + Mn) are selling MANGOES in FAIR.

46.	– Alloy	Al + Mg + Cu + Ni
	Word	**PMS**
		Gambler
	Cu (Copper)	Cup
	Al + Mg +	All Maggie
	Ni (Nickel)	K-nicker

Visualisation:
CUP.

47.	Nichrome	Fe + Ni + Mn + Cr
	Word	**PMS**
	Nichrome	Knee of crome colour
	Fe + Ni	Fenny
	Mn (Manganese)	Mango
	Cr (Cromium)	Crow

Visualisation: MANGOES is growing in FENNY, crow ate, so his KNEE became of CROME COLOUR.

Visualisation: FEW MEN are pulling a CAR, which is full of STEEL MANGOES.

48.	Hostelly c nichrome	Ni + Cr
	Word	**PMS**
	Nichrome	Knee + crome colour
	Cr (Cromium)	Crow
	Hostelloy	Hostel
	Ni (Nickel)	Knicker

Visualisation: In HOSTEL, my KNEE became of CROME COLOUR. Therefore, a CROW is wiping it with KNICKER.

49.	Manganese steel	Fe + Mn + C
	Word	**PMS**
	Manganese	Mangoes of steel
	Fe + Mn	Few men
	C (Carbon)	Car

SOME IMPORTANT PROCESS

1.	Lowig process	NaoH
2.	Pidgeon process	Cl_2

4. Goldschmidt process   Thermite welding

5. Pattinson's process   Ag

In order to memorise the important process, we need to make relation between them.

1. Lowig process   NaOH

Word	PMS
Lowig	Low
NaOH (Caustic soda)	Soap

Visualisation: I am selling SOAP at LOW rate.

2. Pidgeon process   Mg

Word	PMS
Pidgeon	Pigeon
Mg (Magnesium)	Maggie

Visualisation: A PIGEON is eating long-long MAGGIE.

3. Salt cake method Cl_2

Word	PMS
Chlorine (Cl)	Clown
Salt cake	Cake of salt
2	Shoes

Visualisation: A CLOWN is making CAKE OF SALT in shape of SHOES .

4. Goldschmidt process   Thermite welding

Word	PMS
Gold Schmidt	Goldsmith
Thermite	Thermos
Welding	Welding

Visualisation: A GOLDSMITH is WELDING THERMOS.

5. Pattinson's process   Ag

Word	PMS
Pottin	Potten (khraoon)
Son	Son
Silver (Ag)	Silver

Visualisation: My SON is wearing POTTEN made of SILVER.

DISCOVERIES

Anderson	Discovery of positron
Teller	Hydrogen bomb

Comprehensive Memory Development Course

Yukawa	Discovery of masson
Mendeleef	Periodic table
Bacon	Gun powder

We can memorise these discoveries easily by fabricating a funny and interesting stories and by joining all the word together.

Anderson	Discovery of positron
Word	**PMS**
Anderson	Ander + son
Positron	Pusy + train

Visualisation: From ANDER my SON brings PUSY and put it in the TRAIN.

Teller	Hydrogen bomb
Word	**PMS**
Teller	Tailor
Hydrogen	Hydrogen bomb

Visualisation: A TAILOR is sitting on HYDROGEN BALLOON and stretching BOMB.

Yukawa	Discovery of masons
Word	**PMS**
Yukawa	You + kawa
Mason	Mess + on

Visualisation: YOU order to KAWA, go and see MESS is ON or not

Mendeleef	Periodic table
Word	**PMS**
Mendeleef	Man + leaf
Periodic	Period

Visualisation: MAN, wearing LEAF, in my PERIOD always sits on TABLE.

Bacon	Gunpowder
Word	**PMS**
Bacon	Baygon spray

Visualisation: A GUN is full of POWDER, I am cleaning it with BAYGON SPRAY.

HYDROGEN SPECTRUM SERIES

1. Lyman series} UV region
2. Balmer series} Visible region
3. Paschen series} IR region
4. Brackett series} IR region
5. Pfund series} IR region

In order to memorise number, series and region we need to make a connection between them.

1. Lyman series}   UVregion

Word	PMS
1	Son
Lyman	Lemon
Ultra Violet	Untra (a girl) + violet

Visualisation: UNTRA is rubbing VIOLET colour LEMON on her face to clean her face.

2. Balmer series   Visible region

Word	PMS
2	Shoes
Balmer	Boomer (chewingum)

Visualisation: When I ate BOOMER, my whole body became invisible but only SHOES were VISIBLE.

3. Paschen series} IR region
4. Bracket series} IR region
5. Pfund series} IR region

Word	PMS
3	Three monkeys of Gandhiji
4	Door
5	Wife
Paschen	Pashchim
Brackett	Racket
Infra red	Irfan + red
P	Parrot
Fund	Fund

Visualisation: IRFAN brought THREE MONKEYS OF GANDHIJI from PASHCHIM. he tied them with the DOOR and began playing RACKET with PARROT. Suddenly IRFAN'S WIFE came and chid him that I brought this PARROT by losing my all FUND then, why do you not take care of it.

TRIAD GROUP

1. 8,9,10 groups are Triad groups

3. Ruthenium, Rhodium, Palladium – second triad group
4. Osmium, Ridium, Platinum – third triad group

In order to memorise these triad groups, we should make the funny association to give them a permanent space in our memory.

1. 8,9,10 groups are triad groups.

Word	PMS
8	Plate
9	Wine
10	Hen
Triad	Riyadh

Visualisation: A big WINE bottle is putting on a big PLATE and a HEN is serving to all the people of RIYADH.

2. Iron, Cobalt, Nickel – First triad group

Word	PMS
Iron	Iron
Cobalt	Bolt
Nickel	knicker
1	Son
Triad	Riyadh

Visualisation: My SON, stole a BOLT of IRON from RIYADH and hide inside the KNICKER.

3. Ruthenium, Rhodium, Palladium – second triad groups

Word	PMS
Ruthenium	Rath
Rhodium	Road
Palladium	Paddle
2	Couple
Triad	Riyadh

Visualisation: A RATH is standing on the ROAD and COUPLES of RIYADH are making to move its PADDLE.

4. Osmium, Iridium, Platinum – Third triad groups.

Word	PMS
Osmium	Osho

Iridium	Ride
Platinum	Plate
3	Three monkeys of Gandhiji
Triad	Riyadh (a place)

Visualisation: OSHO is RIDING in RIYADH taking a PLATE, in which THREE MONKEYS OF GANDHIJI are sitting.

Chapter 8

MEMORISING FACTS OF BIOLOGY

1. What is the most important factor for the success of animal population?
   – adaptability

   PMS

   Adaptability   adopting

Visualisation: Visualise animals **adopting** baby animals and hence increasing their population.

2. In coming years, skin related disorders will be more common due to
   – depletion of ozone layer

   PMS

   Depletion   deep lotion

   Ozone   zone

Visualisation: Visualise a girl is using **deep lotion** to give shine to some of the **zone** of her skin but skin got disordered because of it.

3. Which one of the following animals is known as a man of the forest?
   – orangeutan   orange

   PMS

   Orangeutan   oranges (a ton)

Visualisation: Visualise an animal looking like a man who is eating **oranges** (a ton) daily in the forest.

4. The most important characteristics of class Aves is
   – Exoskeleton of feathers

   PMS

   Class Aves   Class in evening

   Exoskeleton feathers   Skeleton on which an axe is hanging and cutting the extra feathers of skeleton

Visualisation: Visualise an **evening class** in which teacher is showing a **skeleton on which an axe is hanging and is cutting extra features of skeleton** this is the most important characteristic of the evening class.

5. The head capsule of cockroach is formed by segments numbering – 8

   PMS

Capsule	capsule
8	plate

Visualisation: Visualise a cockroach holding a **plate** on its head in which **capsules** are lying.

6. True Coelom is covered by – Mesoderm.

   PMS

Coelom	coal – lamp
Mesoderm	miss (lady) - dar (fear)

Visualisation: Visualise a lamp made of coals and a **miss** who has a **dar** (fear) is picking it up.

7. oxygen liberated during photosynthesis comes from – Water

   PMS

Oxygen	Ox in Zen

Visualisation: Ox is in zen and taking photo of water scene.

8. The main difference between chlorophyll a and b is that chlorophyll 'a' – Has methyl group whereas chlorophyll b has – CHO group

   PMS

Chlorophyll	Colourful
Methyl	Mitha(sweet)
a	Apple
b	Ball
CHO	chauka(4 Runs)

Visualisation: Visualise yourself playing cricket with a colourful **mitha** (sweet) **apple** as a **ball** and hitting a **chauka** (4 Runs)

9. Calvin cycle – Does not depend on light

   PMS

Calvin	Kelvin refrigerator
Cycle	Cycle

Visulisation: Visulaise that you have won **Kelvin refrigerator** that emits light and hence it does not depend on light.

Comprehensive Memory Development Course

10. Kranz type of anatomy is found in the leaves of – C4 plants

PMS

Kranz	Karna (brother of pandavas)
Anatomy	Tomy (dog)
C4	car (4-r)

Visualisation: Karna and **Tomy** are lying in a car.

Q.1 To memorise disease and their agents:

	Disease	Agent
1.	Elephantaisi	plasmodium
2.	Cysticercosis	
3.	Amoebiasis	entamoeba

1. PMS

Elephantiasis	elephant
Plasmodium	plas – (mouth) dam

Visualisation: An **elephant** is locking **muh** (mouth) of a **dam** with a pilas (tightening device)

2. PMS

Cysticercosis	crystal
Liver	liver 52 (tonic)

Visualisation: Visualise a person playing a   made up of crystal and drinking liver – 52

3. PMS

Amoebiasis	amoeba sitting on ass
Entaamoeba	amoeba sitting on an ant

Visualisation: Visualise an **amoeba sitting on an ass** talking to another **amoeba who is sitting on an ant**.

Q.2 Memorising harmones and their effects?

	Hormones	effect
1.	Melatonin	
2.	MSH	pigment dispersal in melanophres

PMS 1

Melatonin	mela (in fare) me Tony Blair
Ovary	

How to Memorise Biology

Visualisation: Visualise that **Tony Blair** in **mela (chunni)** there.   **odhni**

PMS 2

Msh	mash
Pigment	pig
Melanophores	Millind Soman – pores

Visualisation: Visualise **Milind Soman** is **mashing** a **pig** and **pores** are appearing on it.

1. Vitamin A – Night Blindness & Xeropthalmia
2. Vitamin B1 – Beri beri
3. Vitamin B3 (Mental Confusion) – Pellagra
4. Vitamin C – Scurvy
5. Vitamin D – Rickets & Osteo Malacia

PMS:

We will learn this from the pictures instantly

Vitamin A (Abbu)

Night blindness	Syrup	thal	mia

Visualise that your Abu (father) having **night blindness** having **xerop** in **thal** and after having it he is saying : **mama "mia"** with happiness.

Vitamin b1

beri beri

Vitamin B3 (Mental Confusion)

Phella

Agra

Visualise that three men are saying **"sabse pehla world me Agra hai"** due to mental confusion.

Vitamin D (Dost)

Rackets (Rickets)   O – Sterio - malasia

Visualise that there are two friends (dost), one having the **rackets** and second having a sterio in **malasia**.

To memorise Chromosome number of some organism

To learn this table, you have to to use PMS and phonetic method.

S.no.	Organism	Number of Chromosome in body cell	PMS
1.	Round worm	2	Shoe
2.	Mosquito	6	Vicks
3.	Frog	26	Nag
4.	Rat	42	Rain
5.	Human beings	46	Raja
6.	Guinea pig	64	Jar
7.		100	Thesis
8.		34	Mare
9.	Garden pea	14	Chair
10.	Maize	20	Bat ball
11.	Rice	24	Nari (lady)
12.	Onion	16	hockey

Visualisation:

1. A worm is wearing the shoes of round shape.
2. Mosquitoes are applying vicks on their face.
3. A frog is there in the mouth of
4. A rat is running in rain.
5. Human beings are standing with their
6. You are collecting pigs in a big jar.

9. You are putting a pea and the chair in a garden.

11. A nari is cooking rice for you.
12. You are hitting an onion with a hockey.

To memorise diagrams

Paramecium – the slipper organisms

Diagram of paramecium

PMS

Paramecium	the slipper organisms looks like a big shoe
Cilia	(stitched)
Lines of cilia	silai line (stitched line)
Peristome	stone brought by pan for shoe sole
Vestibule	stone became waste (not required)
Cytophyrynx	sites (place) got torn
Pellicle	yellow nail
Basal granule	grains
Trichocysts	trickey cites
Coudal tuft of cilia	tough
Contractile vacuole	contractor
Opening of contractile	
Vacuole	opened (contractor)

Tributary canal	canal
Food particle	food
Endoplasm	end
Ecto plasm	action
Food vacuole	food hole
Macro nucleus	big new keel (nail)
Micro nucleus	small new (nail)
Tributary canal	additional canal

Visualisation: A very big shoe was stitched and lines of stiching are seen all around the shoe and a stone was brought by a   to attach it in the sole but it was wasted (not required), so a

contractor of the shoe maker opened a canal to store food. Hole was made with a new   (nail) (big and small) and this hole was called as additional canal by the contractor.

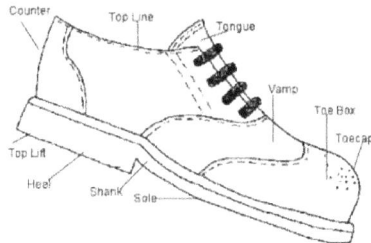

Diagram of a shoe

Chapter 9

MEMORISING THE DIFFERENCE BETWEEN A JOINT COMPANY & A PARTNERSHIP

S.no.	Basis distinction	Partnership	Joint stock company
1.	Law	The indian partnership act 1932 applies	The companies act 1956 applies
2.	No. of members	The minimum is twenty (20) but in case of a banking business, it is ten (10)	In case of a public company, the minimum number is seven (7)without any maximum limit. A private company must have at least two (2) members
3.	Entity	A partnership does not have a separate legal entity	The entity of joint stock company is different from that of its members; it has a separate legal entity
4.	Liability	The liability of partners is unlimited	The liability of members is usually limited to the amount due on the shares held by them.
5.	Capital	There are no restrictions on the	A company cannot have a larger capital than what is authorised by its memorandum; this however, can be increased from time to time. The capital once collected, cannot return without following prescribed procedures.

6.	Distribution of	to the terms of the partnership deed, or equally if there is no agreement	It depends on the Article of Association or the directors as given to the shareholder.
7.	Management	Normally, every partner take part in the management of the affairs	Management is entrusted to the elected directors who must be at least three in number and only two in case of a private company, Shareholders have a right to company at a meeting.
8	Transfer	A partner has no right of transferring his share in the capital to any other person without the consent of other partners. Even on the death of a partner, his heirs do not automatically become partners	Except in case of private companies normally, there are no restrictions on the transfer of shares
9	Audit	Audit is not compulsory unless stated in the partnership deed. However, under the Income Tax Law, audit is compulsory, if the turnover exceeds the prescribed limits.	Under the companies Act, 1956, audit of the accounts of a company is compulsory
10.	Books	If the turn over exceeds the prescribed limits under the Income Tax Law, only the maintenance of books is compulsory.	A company must maintain proper books required under the law, called statuory books.
11.	Business	A partner can carry on any business, if all partners agree.	A company can carry on only that business which is stated in the objects clause of the Memorandum of Association
12	Winding up	A partnership may be wound up by agreement or by an order unable to pay its debts.	A company can be wound up only by carrying out the process laid down in the Companies Act.
13	The Insolvency of all the Act apply Insolvency of all the Partners	The Insolvency of all the Act apply Insolvency of all the Partners.	The Insolvency Act does not apply. Winding up of an insolvent company does not make its members insolvent.

14	Managerial remuneration	There is no restriction under the partnership Act, However, Income Tax Act, 1961 has prescribed the maximum salary.	Managerial remuneration is governed by the companies Act, 1956.
15	Filling of returns	A partnership is not required except the Income Tax Returns	loss account and some other returns annually with the Registrar of companies, so those members of the public can examine them, as well as, the Memorandum and the Aricle of Association.

You visualise the numerical code now with phonetic system and associate the content of

1. **PMS**

1	Tie
Law	Lawyer
Partnership	Partner's Ship
Joint Stock	Socks
32	Moon
56	Lodge

Visualisation: Visualise a **lawyer** wearing tie boarded his **partner's Ship** reserve for moon. Then he wore **socks** and went to a **lodge**.

2. **PMS**

2	ENO
Members	men behind bars
Partnership	partner's ship
20	bat ball
Banking	bank
Public	see lots of men
Joint stock	socks
Private	vet
Seven	heaven
50	lace

Visualisation: You and your partner give **eno** to **men behind bars** and they give you a **bat ball** in return. You deposit it in **bank** to a hen and **see that lots of men** are there wearing **socks** and waiting to go to **heaven** to meet a **vet** and give him a **lace**.

Comprehensive Memory Development Course

3. **PMS**

3	Maa
Entity	t.t
Partnership	partner's ship
Legal	eagle
Joint stock	sock

Visualisation: Visualise you and your partner are not playing **T.T** separately, but with **Maa** and you cannot be separate. Suddenly an **eagle** comes with a pair of **socks** and starts separating.

4. **PMS**

4	ray
Liability	library
Partnership	partner's ship
Stock	sock
Share	lion (sher)

Visualisation: There is a **ray** of light in the **library** where unlimited partners are sitting. Some limited partner are putting **socks** on the *sher*, which are held by them.

5. **PMS:**

5-	hall
Capital	cap
Partnership	partner's ship
Joint stock	socks
Authorised	author
Memorandum	memory pen

Visualisation: You go to a **hall** and give a **cap** to your **partner** and he gives you **lots of money**. With that, you buy **socks** and give it to an **author**. The author gives you a **memory pen** and tells you, the procedure of its working.

6. **PMS:**

6-	jaw
Equality	quails
Joint stock	socks

Visualisation: You and your partner are distributing **jaw** to people in **quails**. They are putting it in **socks** and going to an association of   .

7. **PMS:**

7-	key

Management	manager eating mint
Elected	election
Three	tree
Share	sher (lion)
Accounting	counting

Visualisation: Visualise **manager is eating mint** and giving **key** to partner. Then he goes to take part in **election** undr a **tree**. His symbol is **sher** (lion) and he is counting **votes**.

8. **PMS:**

8-	fee
Consent	saint
Heirs	hair
Private	vet

Visualisation: You pay **fee** for the transfer of your partner because he has become **saint** with long **hair**, green socks. You send him to a **vet**, who puts no restrictions on him.

9. **PMS**

9-	bee
Audit	audio C.D
Deed	will
Income tax law	income tax lawyer
Turnover	turnip
56	lichi

Visualisation: A **bee** sits on the **audio C.D** of your partner and writes a **will** and gives to the **income tax lawyer**

10. **PMS:**

10-	dosa
Partnership	partner
Statutory	statue

Visualisation: If you and your **partner** turn the books, like **dosa** then only they will be maintained. If you clean with socks they will become **statue**.

11. **PMS:**

11-	dad
Objects clause	Santa Clause
Memorandum	memory pen

Visualisation: Your **dad** is going to start a business, if you agree with your partner to write about it on a shocks of the **Santa Clause** with a **memory pen**.

12. **PMS:**

12-	den
Winding	wind
Debts	date
Companies act	acting company

Visualisation: In a **windy den** you sit with your partner who has got **a date** from court because he has stolen socks from an **acting company**.

13. **PMS:**

13	dam
Insolvency	insulin

Visualisation: You bring **insulin** from a **dam** and apply it on your partner but he does not apply on his socks.

14. **PMS:**

14-	deer
Rumuneration	lots of money
61	
56	lodge

Visualisation: With lots of money, a **deer** buys maximum amount of **Chaat** and stores it in a sock of the acting company that is performing a **lodge**.

15. **PMS:**

15-	tail
Balance	see balance of the shop
Register	register
Memorandum	memory pen

Visualisation: You put **a tail** in   and give it as your income tax returns. They put it in a sock and weigh it on **a balance** and then make entry in the picture **register** with a **memory pen** belonging to their association.

Question: What are the steps of selection process of an employee?

Answer: Generally the following steps are used in the selection employee

1. **Requisition:**
   and the type of workers needed in different departments. This is to be done by personal department.

2. **Scrunity of application:** Applications are received in response to advertisement or from other sources. They are scrutinised in the light of requirement and suitability and those found unsuitable are dropped.

3. **Preliminary interview:** Candidates are called for a brief interview in which over all suitability is judged just by their appearance and by putting them between some guerrilaa questions. It is scrrening device to call (for written test) only those candidates who are found suitable.

4. **Application blank:** Candidates found suitable on the basis of preliminary interview are

   the previous job held, and names of references etc.

5. **Checking references:** References may be collected from previous employers, well

6. **Trade and other test:** For technical jobs a candidate may be put to the necessary test to ascertain his ability to work. This test is held under the supervision of a responsible senior person like a supervisor, or a foreman. Other tests such as aptitude test, intelligence test,

   candidates.

7. **Employment interview:**
   job is directly judged by experts or specialists in the board of selection. Only relevant questions relating to the job are asked to elicit required information. In this interview a candidate is fully judged for his communication skills, personality traits, mannerism and overall personality.

8. **Medical test:** Candidates may be asked to get themselves thoroughly examined by a prescribed doctor within the organisation. Such a test detects physical and mental weaknesses that may render them unsuitable for the job.

9. **Induction:** After the candidate is found suitable on the basis of tests and interviews, some orientation is necessary. He may be put to work with his fellow workers to learn the

10. **Placement:**

    Proper placement is necessary to eliminate waste, to increase productivity and to provide work satisfaction.

To memorise these 10 points of selection process you have to use peg method and also use PMS for the key words, join them with the help of chain method.

First take all the 10 points, link them with their number, through peg method and PMS. The 10 points are as follows:

Peg	Word	PMS	PMS link with peg
1. Sun	Requisition	Quiz	Visulaise quiz on sun
2. Shoe	Scrunity of application	Security guard	Visualise special type of shoes worn by security guard

3. Tree	Preliminary interview	See people sitting for interview holding lemon in their hands	Visualise people sitting under a tree holding lemon in their hand for interview
4. Door	Application	A blank application form	See a blank application form pasted on your door
5. Knife	Checking reference	Checking referees	See referees are standing in a line and you are checking them with a knife.
6. Vicks	Trade and other test	Test in trade fair	You are applying vicks on the test papers which are given to you in trade fair.
7. Heaven	Employment interview	Employment newspaper	Through employment newspaper you have got employment in heaven
8. Plate	Medical test	See doctor	Visualise a doctor sitting in a plate
9. Wine	Induction	Duck	Duck drinking wine
10. Hen	Placement	Palace of mint	Visualise a hen sitting in a palace of mint.

Now you can recall all the 10 points in one go. I test you now if I ask you what is point no. 8? You will immediately say – 8 in plate and it is doctor (PMS). It is the medical test.

If I ask you point 5. You will say 5 knife, yes checking refree with knife (PMS), the actual words are checking reference'. Now of course, you can check yourself that how fast you learnt this.

Now from each point you may pick up 3-4 keywords, underline them and make their PMS, and then with the help of the chain method link them with the main heading.

1. **Requisition:**

and type of workers needed in different departments. This is to be done by personal department.

Keywords and PMS

Keywords	PMS
Requisition	we have already made this – quiz
No. of vacancies	vacant places
Department	departmental store
Personal department	your own department store

Visualisation: Visualise you **your own personal departmental store** where a **quiz** is going on, and the **vacant places**   **departmental store**.

How to Memorise LongAnswers of MBA Syllabus

2. **Scrutiny of applications:** Applications are received in response to advertisement or from other sources. They are scrutinised in the light of requirement and suitability and those found unsuitable are dropped.

   PMS:

   Scrutiny   security guard

Visualisation: Visualise the **security guard** is receiving the applications; he throws light on the application. Those who are suitable he keeps them others he drops.

3. **Preliminary interview:** Candidates are called for a brief interviews in which over all suitability is judged by their appearance and by putting them between some gurrillla questions. It is screening device to call (for written test) only those candidates who are found suitable.

   PMS:

   Preliminary   lemon

Visualisation: You can just visualise that people holding **lemon** in their hands are sitting for interview. Those who have big lemons are selected and are called for written test

4. **Application blank:** Candidates found suitable on the basis of preliminary interview are

   the previous job held, and names of references, etc.

Visualisation: You can just visualise whatever is written in this point, no need to make PMS.

5. **Checking references:** References may be collected from previous employers, well

   PMS:

   Reference   referee

Visualisation: Visualise a **referee** is collecting the previous references from different people

6. **Trade and other test:** For technical jobs a candidate may be put to the necessary test to ascertain his ability to work. This test is held under the supervision of a responsible senior person like a supervisor, or a forema. Other tests such as aptitude test, intelligence test,

   candidates.

   PMS:

                                      fair

Visualisation: In **trade fair** you are appearing for various tests like aptitude test, ability test, personality test etc., under the supervision of supervisor or foreman.

7. **Employment interview:**

   job is directly judged by experts or specialists in the board of selection. Only relevant questions relating to the job are asked to elicit required information. In this interview a candidate is fully judged for his communication skills, personality traits, mannerism and overall personality.

Visualisation: Visualise yourself reading employment newspaper, you are judged by experts and they also ask you relevant questions. Manners and overall personality is also judged.

8. **Mental test:** Candidates may be asked to get themselves thoroughly examined by a prescribed doctor within the organisation. Such a test detects physical and mental weaknesses that may render them unsuitable for the job.

   PMS:

   Visualisation:
   not.

8. **Induction:** After the candidate is found suitable on the basis of tests and interviews some orientation is necessary. He may be put to work with his fellow workers to learn the

   PMS:

   | Placement | palace of mint |

Visualisation: Visualise that the duck has entered a new job, she is following what her fellow

10. Placement:

Proper placement is necessary to eliminate waste, to increase productivity and to provide work satisfaction.

Visualisation: Finally, you enter into a palace full of mint, you are looking for the right place to get seated, when you are properly placed you throw all the waste of the palace, increase the productivity of mint and provide work satisfaction to the people.

Chapter 10

MEMORISING RECIPROCALS

1. **Reciprocal of 28 is 0.0357.** Here, ignore the zero, since it appears in all the reciprocals. Now convert 357 into a peg word.

    MLK – MILK. The peg word for 28 is Knife. Now associate knife and milk. You have got the reciprocal for 28.

Visualisation: You are having milk while doing so you are cutting vegetables with knife also.

2. **The reciprocal of 9 is 0.111.** You can remember them by associating bee (9) with DDT (.111).

Visualisation: You are killing bees with spraying DDT.

3. **The reciprocal of 11 is 0.0909.** Associate Daddy (11) with Busy Bee (.909).

Visualisation: Visualise that your daddy is playing with bees.

MEMORISING SQUARES, CUBE ROOTS AND CUBE (ASSOCIATE BY YOURSELF)

1. **The square root of 10 is 3.162.** Convert them into peg words and associate 'Dosa' (10) with Ma (3) and touch in (162).

Visualisation: Visualise that you are having Dosa with Ma and Ma is touching you.

2. **The square root of 21 is 4.58.** Convert them into peg words and associate net (21) with Ray (4) and Leaf (58).

Visualisation: Visualise that a ray coming through a net is falling upon a leaf.

3. **The square root of 30 is 5.477.** Convert them into peg words and associate Mouse (30) with Lawyer (54) and raw cake (477).

Visualisation: Visualise that a mouse is with a lawyer as it is his pet and has a raw cake.

4. **The cube root of 2 is 1.26.** Convert them into peg words and associate Knee (2) with Tie (1) and Naach (26) or Nisha (any known girl of this name).

Comprehensive Memory Development Course

Visualisation: Visualise that your knee is injured while dancing and you tied it with a tie and again you start dancing (nach) with your partner nisha.

5. **The cube root of 3 is 1.44.** Convert them into peg words and associate ma (3) with Tie (1) and Rear (44).

Visualisation: Visualise that your Ma is tying a tie in you neck and showing you in a rear mirror of the car that 'you are looking nice'.

6. **The cube root of 9 is 2.08.** Convert them into peg words and associate Bee (9) with Knee (2) and sofa (08) or Fee.

Visualisation: Visualise that a bee bites your knee and you are taking rest on sofa.

7. **The cube root of 21 is 2.75.** Convert them into peg words and associate Net (21) with knee (2) and Kela (75).

Visualisation: Visualise that your knee is trapped in a net while eating   .

8. **The cube root of 29 is 3.072.** Convert them into peg words and associate Nib (29) with Ma (3) and Skin (072) or with Mouse (30) and Gun (72)

Visualisation: Visualise that you are giving a Nib to Ma to kill the mouse while putting nib in a gun.

9. **The cube of 12 is 1728.** Associate Don (12) with Toffee and Knife (1728).

Visualsation: Visualise that a Don is cutting a toffee with knife.

10. **The cube of 16 is 4096.** Associate dish (16) with Rose Beach (4096)

Visualisation: Visualise that you are having a dish on beach full of roses.

11. **The cube of 29 is 24389.** Associate Nib (29) with Noorie Move up (24389)

Visualisation: Visualise that you are writing a song (noorie) with Nib and saying noorie to move up.

How to Memorise Mathematics

Chapter 11

MEMORISING ACCOUNTING STANDARD

AS-1   disclosure of accounting policies

AS-2   valuation of inventories

AS-4   contingencis for events occurring after the balance sheet date

AS-6   depriciation accounting

AS-7   construction contracts

AS-8   research and development cost

AS-9   revenue recognition

AS-11   accounting for the effects of change in foreign exchange rates

AS-12   governement grants

AS-13   accounting for investments

AS-14   accounting for amalgation

AS-16   borrowing costs

AS-17   segment reporting

AS-18   related party disclosures

AS-19   leases

AS-20   earning per share

AS-22   accounting for taxes on income

To memorise these you have to visualise AS as "ass" and 1 as "sun". AS-2 as an "shoe". AS-3 as " tree" and so on. Now, you have to see the link between AS-1 and statement. From the

AS-1   disclosure of accounting policies

PMS:

AS-1   sun

Policies   police

Visualisation: Visualise a **policeman** standing under sun with an **ass** to disclose his   accounts.

AS-2   valuation of inventories

PMS:

AS-2   shoe

Inventories   invention

Visualisation: Visualise an ass **inventing** his own **shoes**.

PMS:

AS-3   tree

Visualisation: Sitting on a **tree**

AS-4   contingencis for events occurring after the balance sheet date

PMS:

AS-4   door

Balance sheet   balance sheet

Visualisation: Some contingency has occurred so an ass standing on **door** is adjusting it in the **balance sheet**.

PMS:

AS-5   knife

Period   class period

Visualisation:

or loss they have gained from this period, and asking the students to change the accounting policies as the net loss was too much.

AS 6   depreciation accounting

PMS:

AS-6   vicks

Depreciation   depression

Visualisation: Visualise an ass applying **vicks** as he is deeply **depressed** after seeing accounts.

AS-7   construction contracts

PMS:

AS-7   heaven

Visualisation: Visualise an ass got a **contract** in **heaven**

AS-8   research and development cost

PMS:

AS-8   plate

Visualisation: Visualise an ass counting **plates** as he is doing research on that.

AS-9   revenue recognition

PMS:

AS-9   wine

Revenue   venue

Visualisation: Visualise an ass willing to drink **wine**, looking for a venue where to sit and drink.

PMS:

AS-10   hen

Fixed assets   see fan/tv/furniture

Visualisation: An ass and **hen** plan to live together so they are collecting **fan / TV/ fridge/ furniture,** etc.

AS-11   accounting for the effects of change in foreign exchange rates

PMS:

AS-11   stick

Foreign exchange   foreigner in exchange

Visualisation: An ass gets a **foreigner in exchange** of his **stick** and he sees the effect of this change.

AS-12   Accounting for governments grants

PMS:

AS-12   duck

Accounting   counting

Visualisation: Visualise an ass is **counting duck**, as he wants to give these **ducks** to the government in grants.

AS-13   Accounting for investments

PMS:

AS-13   heart

Accounting   counting

Invest   in waste

Visualisation: Visualise an ass **counting heart** (balloons in shape of heart) and keeping them **in his waste**.

AS-14	accounting for amalgation

PMS:

AS-14	chair
Accounting	counting
Amalgation	amul butter

Visualisation: Visualise an ass **counting** chair and on each chair he is placing **amul butter**.

PMS:

AS-15	hook
Retirement	a retired person

Visualisation: Visualise an ass is holding **a retired person** with **hook**.

AS-16	borrowing costs

PMS:

AS-16	hockey

Visualisation: An ass is **borrowing** a **hockey** and paying cost for it to you.

AS-17	segment reporting

PMS:

AS-17	lamp
Segment	(spinach) with mint

Visualisation: Visualise an ass standing under a **lamp** and mixing mint in *saag*.

AS-18	related party disclosures

PMS:

AS-18	spectacles
Party	visualise a of party

Visualisation: Visualise an ass wearing **spectacles** in **party**.

AS-19	leases

PMS:

AS-19	lolly pop
Lease	leaves

Visualisation: Visualise an ass eating **lollypop** made up of **leaves**.

AS-20	earning per share

PMS:

AS-20	bat and ball

| Share | sher (lion) |

Visualisation: An ass has increased his earning by playing **bat and ball** with a   (lion)

PMS:

| AS-21 | net (emailing) |
| Consolidated | counsellor |

Visualisation: **net** (emailing)

| AS-22 | accounting for taxes on income |

PMS:

| AS-22 | nana (grandfather) |
| Income Tax | incoming taxi |

Visualisation: An ass counting incoming taxis with his **nana** (grandfather).

MEMORISING THE AUDIT MANAGEMENT

Q 1: Write a short note on Management note?

Ans:

performance and effectiveness of management of an organisation. It is a thorough going, critical and constructive review of the quality of management and is generally conducted at the instance of top management. The audit work is generally done by an independent team of experts from relevant areas. They naturally adopt some of the tried and tested principles of auditing. The aim is to make an objective assessment of the manner in which the affairs of the organisation are managed. The audit is conducted on a periodic basis. The audit team collects evidence from historical records about the various aspects of the functioning of the organisation. It may also generate data through questionnaires circulated among the members of the management team, the other members of the organisation and a representative cross-section of the client goups. The audit team forms its opinions and conclusions on the basis of analysis of the evidence and information so collected and generated against a set of relevant criteria of performance and effectiveness if possible. The opinions and conclusions so arrived at could take the form of recommendations for future guidance of management and could form the basis for reform of the process and practices of management of the organisation in question.

PMS:

KEYWORD	PMS
Management	manager
Audit	body
	deaf
Systematic evaluation	(music) system of value

Functioning	function
Performance	foreman
Effectiveness	a fatty nurse
Review	river
Quality	Kwality ice cream
Top management	topping on ice cream
Independent	independence day
Team of experts	picture team of 4-5 people from CBI
Process	recess
Tested principles	picture that principal of your college being tested
Objective	object (jack)
Assessment	ass+ass = 2 ass
Affairs	fair
Periodic	
Evidence	den
Historical records	story is recorded
Questionnairs	questions
Opinion	onion
Analysis	sister Ana
Recommendation	rack +mend (mending the broken rack)
Reform	form

Visualisation: Visualise a manager of a company. That manager is very fat. He has a very heavy body. The manger is deaf also.

Visualse that the manager has got a music system of high value (very costly). Because the manager is deaf, you purchase the music system from him by paying the value. With this music system in hand, you go to attend the marriage function. There you see a foreman of the company dancing on the stage. He falls down and hurts his leg. A fatty nurse comes there to mend his leg. You help the nurse. She is happy with you. She takes you to the river and gives you Kwality ice cream of vanilla favour. You put chocolate topping on the ice cream. You are walking while eating the ice cream and you notice that at near distance some people are

team of experts from CBI is celebrating this Independence Day.

You saw that in that function many principals from different colleges are standing there

are given a jack (used to lift a car) which they have to break into two parts. The judges are two asses.

You go and sit on one ass and the ass takes you to the fair. In the fair you meet one   and she takes you to a den in the jungle. In the den a person is telling a story. You record the story. After completing that story, the person asks you questions about the story. You answer correctly. So he gives you an onion as a prize.

You cut the onion and from that onion, sister Ana comes out crying. She is crying because her rack has broken and she wants you to mend it. You say o.k. after that rack has been mended; she gives you a form which says that you are the best person in the world.

You are reading the form and suddenly a bell rings indicating that the recess is over. You realise that you fell asleep during the recess and that was a dream.

Q 2: Explain the factors that determine the span of management.

Ans:

1. **Nature and importance of work:** If the work under reference is of routine and standard type, the span can be safely widened. On the other hand, if the work is risky and complicated, the same would require tight supervision, and the span of management would be essentially narrow.

2. **Competence of managers:** If the managers are competent enough, they can handle and control a fairly large number of subordinates otherwise, the span should be necessarily narrow.

3. **Ability of subordinates:** If the subordinates are educated and experienced, they would need normal supervision and control, and the span of management can be quite wide. In case of uneducated and inexperienced workers, the span should be necessarily narrow.

4. **Availability of time:**
   to be narrow, which is true of top management. The span can be wide in case of lower management who have relatively more time at their disposal.

5. **Availability of specialists:** In the event of availability of specialists, the span can be wide because there would be little problems and complexities to grapple with. In the absence of such specialists, the manager's task remains demanding, and the span would be consequently narrow.

6. **Organisational planning:** If the planning is elaborate and detailed, large number of subordinates can be easily supervised by a single superior otherwise the span would be narrow.

7. **System of control:** If observation has been adopted as a method of control, the span should be necessarily narrow. If impersonal techniques are followed, the span can be wide.

8. **Communication:** If the communication system is effective the span can be wide.

9. **Delegation of authority:** If there is a system of delegation of authority, the span of management can be wide otherwise it would be narrow.

10. **Team spirit among employees:** If the employees are spirited and enthusiastic, they woud require little supervision and control, hence the span would be wide.

Comprehensive Memory Development Course

Now we will try to learn these points with the help of PMS and association.

KEYWORD	PMS
Span of management	of manager
Nature and importance of work	, import, worbook
Competence of managers	computer of manager
Ability of subordinates	(cat), board
Availability of time	clock
Specialists	special lists
Planning	plane
Control	cream roll
Communication	common cat
Delegation of authority	Delhi, auto
Team spirit	bottle of spirit

Visualise the picture of manager eating   and driving a tractor.

1. Visualise your manager eating paan. Manager's name is Nattu and he imports drawing work books from the sun. He brings these work books from the sun

2. Visualise that manager is using the shoe instead of a mouse to operate the computer.

3. A   (cat) is sitting on a huge tree with a big board and teaching A- B- C-D to (other animals) the manager.

4. You are trying to stick the clocks on your door with the help of   instead of fevicol.

5. You are cutting the special lists containing pictures of different kinds of   with a big knife.

6. You are applying vicks on the whole plane, carrying   from one country to other, so that it doesn't catch cold because of the winter season.

7. All the gods and goddessess in the heaven are eating cream rolls rolled in   .

8. Your manager is very happy with your work. So he gifts you a cat but it is a very common cat. To make it look different you stick steel plates containing different pictures of   on its ears. Now it is not a common cat. It is a unique cat.

9. In Delhi, auto drivers use wine instead of petrol for their auto.

10. The Indian cricket team has won the match and the chief guest Hen, with a   in her mouth, is awarding a bottle of spirit to all the team members.

If you read the answer carefully, you will realise that if you remember these representative words or important points, then explaining them in detail is very easy.

Responsibility of the Auditor in consideration of Laws & Regulations in an Audit of Financial Statement. SA (Standards on Auditing)-250

SAs are designed to assist the auditor in identifying material misstatement of the

However, the auditor is not responsible for preventing non-compliance & can't be expected to detect non-compliance with all laws & regulations.

SA distinguishes the Auditor's responsibilities in relation to compliance with two different categories of laws & regulations as follows :

(a)   The Provisions of those laws & regulations have a direct effect on the material

about the compliances.

(b)   For other laws & regulations that don't have a direct effect on the amounts &

Visualisation:

Visualise as chairman of CA institute has designed an SA (Standard on Auditing) & the auditor is reading that SA, that SA helps the auditor in this way: After reading SA auditor audits the Financial Statement of a company & gets a paper which is

Now another Blank paper which shows non-compliance is skipped by the auditor

auditor because he is not responsible for detection of non-compliance.

(a) Then auditor goes to another room in which there are some papers. Auditor takes

to put some weight on papers so he puts a camera on those papers which is a symbol of appropriate audit evidence.

(b) Visualise as auditor has put his left hand on some papers which are on the table,

visualise as auditor is performing a rigorous checking.

Explain Joint Auditor, why they are appointed, their basis of division of work & their Separate & Joint Responsibilities.

Joint Auditor– When two or more Practicing units are appointed to conduct audit of an entity.

Why: Due to voluminous work in large entities.

Basis of Division of work: they divide work among themselves on the basis of:-
        Period

        Geographical location, etc.

Responsibilities:

Separate: work allocated.

Own audit programs drafted.

Keeping appropriate documentation.

Joint:

Audit work not divided.

Collective decisions on audit programs.

Visualisation: Visualise 4-5 CA having joint hands & one pen in another hand symbolising joint audit. Now, visualise all CAs are entering in a company in which papers are so much that they are touching the roof, which symbolises due to voluminous work joint audit is required.

Basis of division of work: Visualise those many papers are divided & put in three boxes, on one box a big table watch is put which symbolises PERIOD, on second box so much cash to

Geographical location.

Responsibilities: Separate: - Visualise all CAs are sitting together & have taken some papers from total papers (allotted some work out of all total work), now they are writing audit program on a paper which they have put in their pocket as a documentation.

Joint: Visualise some papers in the middle of all of them which are still not divided, on them all taking collective decisions on audit program, visualise all are writing on those undivided papers. Then they are disclosed by all of them symbolising disclosure requirements of all joint responsibilities.

Inspection: Examining records, documents or tangible assets.

Observation: Witnessing a process or procedure being performed by others.

Inquiry consists of seeking appropriate information from

response to an inquiry.

Recalculation: checking mathematical accuracy of documents or records.

Visualisations: Visualise an auditor is examining papers, of tangible assets like computer, chair, table, etc. to assure that what is written in records actually exists.

Now, Auditor goes to Stock department where he observes the counting of stocks performed by others (client's employees).

After observing auditor asks (inquires) from the knowledgeable person sitting near him, who

After getting the response auditor takes the calculator & recalculate the amounts shown in the records to check the mathematical accuracy.

Chapter 12

Lets discuss how you can memorise general knowledge questions for civil services/competitive examination.

1. The parliamentary system of government in India is based on the pattern of Parliamentary Government in
   a. Great Britain
   b. France
   c. USA
   d. Canada

Ans: a.

Visualisation:

2. Which of the following is described as the soul of the constitution?
   a. Fundamental rights
   b. Directive principles of state policy
   c. Power of judicial review enjoyed be the supreme court
   d. Preamble

Ans: d.

PMS: Preamble   prem (love ka ball)

       Constitution   constable

       Soul   sole of shoes

Visualisation: A constable is hitting a   (heart shaped) ball with the sole of shoes.

3. Who is legally competent to declare war or conclude peace
   a. The president
   b. The council of ministers

c. The parliament

d. The prime ministers

Ans: a.

Visualisation: Our president is the only person who is gone for a war and if he won it there was complete peace.

4. How many types of emergencies are envisaged by the constitution?

a. None

b. 2

c. 3

d. 4

Ans: 3

PMS: 3   tree (in rhyme method)

Constitution   constable

Emergency   emergency toilet

Visualisation: whenever a constable has to go for emergency toilet he goes behind the tree.

a. Once

b. Twice

c. Thrice

d. Never

Ans: d.

Visualisation: Our president is addressing all people saying that there is abundant money and

6. The prime minister is

a. Elected by Lok Sabha

b. Elected by the two houses of parliament at a joint sitting

c. Appointed by the president

d. Elected by the Lok Sabha and appointed by the president

Ans: Appointed by the president

PMS: PM   Manmohan Singh

President   Pranab Mukharjee

Visualisation: Visualise, Manmohan Singh is being appointed as PM again by the new president, Pranab Mukharjee.

7. Which one of the following states has a separate constitution
   a. Jammu and Kashmir
   b. Nagaland
   c. West Bengal
   d. A and b both

Ans: Jammu and Kashmir

PMS: constitution   constable

        Jammu and Kashmir   terrorists

Visualisation: Terrorists are killing constable and forming their separate group of constables.

8. The Sarkaria Commission favoured

   b. Selection of governer of a state by the president from a panel of names given by the concerned states government

   d. None of the above

Ans:

PMS: Sarkaria   sir ki kar (car)

        Governor   governor general

Visualisation: Visualise that a general will charge commission, if you want to take

9. The quorum, or minimum number of members required to hold the meeting of either house of parliament is
   a. One fourth of total membership of the house

   c. One third of total membership of the house
   d. One tenth of total membership of the house

Ans: d.

PMS: quorum   queue for rum

        One tenth   one teeth

Visualisation: There are many rooms in parliament, so it was decided that if meeting is supposed to be held then please stand in a queue and ask for rum and take one teeth from every member.

10. The president can nominate two members of the Lok Sabha to represent the
    a. Anglo-Indians

b. India Christians

c. Buddhists

d. Parsees

Ans: a.

PMS:	Lok sabha	logo ki sabha (persons meeting)
	Two	shoe (in rhyme)
	Anglo Indians	angry Indians
	President	Pranab Mukharjee

Visualisation: Pranab Mukharjee asked in _____ to take out shoes of all angry Indians

11. Who is the supreme commander of the armed forces of india?

a. the president

b. the prime minister

c. the defence minister

d. none of the above

Ans: a.

PMS:	supreme	supreme's chair
	President	APJ Abdul Kalam

Visualisation: The APJ Abdul kalam is talking to all commanders sitting on supreme chair of armed forces in india.

12. Which one of the following was elected president of india unopposed?

a. Dr. Rajinder Prasad

b. Dr. S Radhakrishnana

c. Dr. Zakir Hussain

d. N Sanjiva Reddy

Ans: d.

PMS:	Sanjiva	Sanjeev Kumar (actor)
	Reddy	ready

Visualisation: Visualise that when Sanjeev Kumar got ready to perform the role of president, no one opposed him.

a. The chief justice of the Supreme Court

b. The attorney general of India

c. Union law minister

d.   None of the above

PMS: attorney

Visualisation:
on his knee.

14. The number of judges of a high court is determined by

a.   The Chief Justice of india

b.   The president of india

c.   The governor of the state

d.   The parliament

Ans: b.

PMS: President   Pranab Mukharjee

Visualisation: Visualise that Pranab Mukharjee is directing to put no. of chairs in the high court, so that judges could sit easily.

15. The doctorine of Lapse was introduced by

a.   Dalhousie

b.   Curzon

c.   Rippon

d.   Lytton

Ans: a.

PMS: doctorine of lapse   doctor collapsed

Dalhousie   Daal- house

Visualisation: A doctor collapsed when he ate   at your house.

16. Mahabalipuram was established by the

a.   Pallavas

b.   Pandyas

c.   Cholas

d.   Chalukyas

Ans: b.

PMS: Mahabalipuram   hanuman puran

Pallavas   pillow

Visualisation: One can read Hanuman Puran, keeping it on only pillows.

17. Who founded four Mathas in the four corners of India?

a.   Shankaracharya

b. Ramanujacharya

c. Bhaskaracharya

d. madhvacharya

Ans: a.

PMS: 4 mathas   4 glasses of matta (diluted curd)

Shankaracharya   Shankar acharya

Visualisation: Shankar sitting with Acharya jee in the centre of India and drinking   from all the 4 corners of India.

18. Upnishads are books on

a. Religion

b. Yoga

c. Philosophy

d. Law

Ans: c.

PMS: Upnishad

Philosophy   pillow + softy

Visualisation: You are writing a book on pillow with softy, in   (your own words).

19. In the Mughal Empire, the unit of land revenue assessment was

a. Individual

b. Parganas

c. Village

d. Zamindar

Ans: c.

PMS: Mughal Empire   ek ghayal mor (an injured peacock)

Visualisation: (an injured peacock) was collecting land revenue from village.

20. Babur introduced in India.

a. The art of Persian painting

b. Royal court poetry

c. Four – square gardens

d. Building with sloping walls

Ans: c.

PMS: Babur   Barber

Four square gardens   four square cigarettes

Visualisation: Barber was cutting hair with a four square cigarettes in his mouth.

MEMORISING VOCABULARY

association. For Example:

S. No.	WORD	MEANING	PMS
1.	Ablution	Washing	Lotion
	Visualisation: washing a blue (PMS for ablution is blue lotion) uniform with lotion.		
2.	Exculpate	To Clear from Blame	Ex Culprit
	Visualisation: A culprit who is being acquitted by a court becomes an ex culprit later.		
3.	Hegemony	Superiority	Hedge
	Visualisation: your superior hiding money in a hedge (long bushes).		
4.	Badger	the fur or hair of the mammal	badge
	Visualisation: A badge made of fur is worn by this mamal.		
5.	Balmy	mild and pleasant	balm
	Visualisation: This balm has such a pleasant smell.		
6.	Besmirch	to make dirty	bees (20), March
	Visualisation: Slip with "20 march" written on it, thrown on the ground, making the whole ground look dirty.		
7.	Black ball	reject or vote against black, ball	
	Visualisation: I do not like this black ball. I vote against it's entry in club.		
8.	Blight	any of numerous plants diseases resulting in sudden conspicuous wilting and dying of affected parts, especially young growing tissues	light
	Visualisation: This young plant needs light to avoid diseases.		
9.	Capsize	to overturn or cause to overturn	cap, size
	Visualisation: The size of your cap is so big that its weight has overturned this boat.		
10.	Abridge	to cut short Curtail	a bridge
	Visualisation: Why did you cut short or curtail this bridge.		
11.	Accord	harmony	a cord
	Visualisation: We agree that this cord can put on the AC.		

Comprehensive Memory Development Course

12.	Adamant	stubbornly, unyielding	an ant
	Visualisation: This ant will not change its mind to quit from this advertisement.		
13.	Affront	to insult intentionally	front
	Visualisation: It is an insulting to always see you in front of the door.		
14.	Agape	Wide open	gap
	Visualisation: I am measuring gap of my wide open mouth with this scale.		
15.	Alimony	a means of livelihood all, money maintenance	
	Visualisation: You give all your money to your ex- wife as a mainteneance for her life.		
16.	Tessellated	to form into a mosaic pattern	tea – salt
	Visualisation: A person is selling tea on a cube with music pattern.		
17.	Temporize	to engage in discussion or negotiations	tempo, price
	Visualisation: I want to negotiate the price of this tempo.		
18.	Tantamount	equivalent in effect or value	tent, amount
	Visualisation: Both these tents amount to same value.		
19.	Covert	not openely practiced or displayed	cover
	Visualisation: displayed.		
20.	Chaff	worthless	chef
	Visualisation: This Chef is worthless. He doesn't even know how to make tomato soup.		
21.	Arrack	a strong alcoholic drink	a rack
	Visualisation: He is having alcoholic drink sitting on a rack.		
22.	Dicey	involving with risk	dice
	Visualisation: I wish to gamble using this dice but it is risky.		
23.	Appall		a pal
	Visualisation: He is my pal. I am shocked to see him taking bribe.		
24.	Flux	continous change	lux
	Visualisation: I think its because of lux, my complexion is continuously changing.		
25.	Bout	a contest between antagonists; a match	out
	Visualisation: I have come out early from school to rush to see wrestling match on TV.		
26.	Tantrum		tent, rum
	Visualisation:		

Here are given some more words, but these times try you to memorise it.

WORD	MEANING
Antagonism	Opposition
Canoe	Light Boat
Canter	Move slowly
Flagon	Vessel of wine
Newt	Kind of lizard
Slip	Mistake
Flurry	Blast of wind
Lather	Soap foam
Mane	Long hair on the neck
Hart	Male dee

MEMORISING COUNTRY, CAPITAL AND CURRENCY

For memorising country name and its capital, associate country's name with capital's name.

Example:

1. The capital of Bulgaria is Sophia.
   Country   **capital**

Now create PMS for both words and after giving them an image, link them (images) together.

   Bulgaria – Bull   (Fell down),
   Sophia – Sofa set

Visualisation: A bull   on the sofa set.

2. The capital of USA is Washington
   Country   **capital**
   USA   Washington
   PMS for USA – use and
   For Washington – Washing

Visualisation: You have used many clothes and you are washing them.

3. The capital of Fiji is Suva.
   Country   **capital**
   Fiji   Suva
   PMS for Fiji can be Fauji or soldiers and
   For Suva – can be a big needle (Suva)

Comprehensive Memory Development Course

Visualisation:
in their hands.

4. The currency of Italy is Lira.

Country	currency
Italy	Lira

   PMS for Italy can be   (a south Indian dish) and
   For Lira – Lada (Fought)

Visualisation: You fought with your sister to get more idly.

5. | Country | Currency |
   | --- | --- |
   | Australia | Dollar |

   PMS:

Australia	kangaroo (a national animal)
Dollar	doll

Visualisation: Visualize that a kangaroo is playing with the doll.

6. | Country | Currency |
   | --- | --- |
   | America | dollar |

   PMS:

America	Mr. America (Rithik Roshan in "Mujhse Dosti Karoge")
Dollar	doll

Visualisation: Visualise that Mr America (Rithik Roshan) is gifting a doll to kKareena Kapoor for playing.

7. | Country | Currency |
   | --- | --- |
   | Armenia | Dram |

   PMS:

Armenia	army men
Dram	drum

Visualisation: Visualise that army mens are beating drum.

8. | Country | Currency |
   | --- | --- |
   | Baharain | dinar |

   PMS:

Baharrain	rain (raining outside)
Dinar	dinner

Visualisation: Visualise that a boy is saying to a girl "   "

9. | Country | Currency |
   | --- | --- |
   | Cyprus | pound |

PMS:

Cyprus	syrup
Pound	pond

Visualisation: Visualise that you are pouring syrup in the pond.

10. **Country**   **Currency**

Ghana   cidi

PMS:

Ghana	(song)
Cidi	CD (compact disk)

Visualisation: Visualise that you are playing a   (song) in a cd.

11. **Country**   **Currency**

Maltese   lira

PMS:

Maltese	malta
Lira	Lara Dattta (actress)

Visualisation: Visualise that Lara Dutta is having malta in milk.

12. **Country**   **Currency**

Botswana   pula

PMS:

Botswana boats in van

Pula   pull

Visualisation: Visualise that you are pulling boats in a van.

13. **Country**   **Currency**

Samoa   tala

PMS:

Samoa	samosa
Tala	(lock)

Visualisation: Visualise that samosa is locked with a tala (lock) that nobody can have it.

14. **Country**   **Currency**

Honduras   lempira

PMS:

Honduras	Honda with
Lempira	lamp

Visualisation:

15. **Country**   **Currency**
    Bermuda   dollar
    PMS:
    Bermuda   Bermuda *(pajama)
    Dollar   doll

Visualisation: Visualse that yor are wearing a Bermuda patched or sticked with a doll.

Now some more words try for yourself:

Country	Currency
Combodia	Riel
Mongolia	Tugrik
Panama	Balboa
Russia	Rubel
Italy	Euro

Likewise you can memorise others by association method.

Multiple choice questions of General Knowledge:

1. Diamond is chemically:
   a.   A mixture of mental carbonates
   b.   Pure carbon
   c.   A pure form of sand
   d.   A mixture of metal carbonate phosphorus

Ans: pure carbon

PMS:
Carbon   carbon paper

Visualisation:

2. The gas inside an electric bulb is:
   a.   Air
   b.   Oxygen
   c.   Nitrogen
   d.   Carbon dioxide

Ans: nitrogen

PMS:
Nitrogen   night rose

Visualisation: At night, you switched on an electric bulb and roses started coming out of it.

3. The acid present in lemons and oranges is
   a. Acetic acid
   b. Hydrochloric acid
   c. Citric acid
   d. Decantation

Ans: citric acid

PMS:

Citric acid   sitter

Visualisation: You are sitting in a baby sitter and eating lemons and oranges.

4. Gobar gas contains mainly
   a. Carbon dioxide
   b. Methane
   c. Acetylene
   d. Ethylene

Ans: methane

PMS:

Gobar gas

Methane   make hen

Visualisation: Gobar is being used to make hen.

5. The term 'ph' denotes the
   a. Temperature of a solution
   b. Vapour pressure of a solution
   c. Acidity or basicity of a solution
   d. Ionic strength of a solution.

Ans: acidity or basicity of a solution

PMS:

PH   pitch

Visualisation:

normal to play cricket.

6. The gas that can be used as a fuel is
   a. Oxygen
   b. Nitrogen
   c. Methane
   d. Fluorine

Ans: methane

PMS:

Gas	stove
Methane	make hen

Visualise: Visualise your gas stove on which you are cooking a full hen.

7. Ammonia is prepared commercially by the
   a. Oswald process
   b. Hall process
   c. Haber process
   d. Contact process

Ans: Haber process

PMS:

Ammonia	(raw mango)
Haber process	(berry)

Visualisation: Ambi is prepared commercially by taking   . (Berry in hand)

8. The process of extracting aluminium is called
   a. Dow process
   b. Haber process
   c. Hall process
   d. Benzic acid

Ans: Hall process

PMS:

Aluminium	mini
Hall process	hall

Visualisation: Lots of mini   are kept in a hall.

9. Coke is produced from luminous coal by
   a. Cracking
   b. Synthesis
   c. Substitution
   d. Destructive distillation

Ans: Destructive distillation

PMS:

Bituminous	Britney spear

Visualisation: Visualise Britney Spear preparing the coke on coal by destructing distillation of water.

10. The chemical 'styrene' is industrially used in the production of
    a. Pharmaceuticals
    b. Dyes
    c. Plastic
    d. Insecticides

Ans: Plastics

PMS:

Styrene   syringe

Visualisation: The syringe is industrially used in the production of plastics.

1. Here are given some River names and their valleys related to them. Try to make PMS and associate them by visualisation.

RIVER	VALLEY
Bhakra	Satluj
Thein	Ravi
Beas	Beas
Sharda	Ghagra
Banasagar	Sone
Hirakund	Mahanadi
Nagarjuna	Krishna
Mettur	Kaveri

2. Here are given some sites and their location. Try to make PMS and associate them by visualisation.

SITE	LOCATION
Amber Palace	Jaipur
Birla Planetorium	Kolkata
Bodhisattva	Ajanta Cave
Buland Darwaja	Fatepur Sikri
Bhakra Dam	Punjab
Charminar	Hyderabad
Dal lake	Srinagar

3. Here are given some lakes and their states. Try to make PMS and associate them by visualisation.

LAKE	STATE
Chilka	Odisha
Dal	Jammu & Kashmir

Kolleru	Andhra Pradesh
Sambhar	Rajashthan
Pullicat	Tamil Nadu
Kayal	Kerala

them by visualisation.

Country	Flower
Canada	Mapple
England	Rose
France	Lily
Germany	
India	Lotus
Ireland	Shemrock

them by vsualisation.

Disease	Body Part
Cataract	Eye
Elephantasis	Leg and feet
Arthritis	Bone and Joint
Hemophilia	Blood
Rikets	Bone
Goitre	Thyroid
Gangrene	Body cell and tissue
Trachoma	Eye
Cheilosis	Mouth
Glucoma	Eye
Anaemia	Blood

PART : III

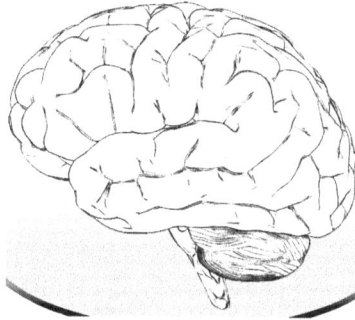

Psycho Neurobic Exercises for Developing The Mind and Memory Power

Chapter 1

1. Blissful sound neurobics
2. Enlightment neurobics
3. Dynamic neurobics
4. Neurobics Spa

BLISSFUL SOUND NEUROBICS (ACTIVATING CROWN CHAKRA)

This Neurobics raises the frequency level in all body cells and tissues up to 732 trillions triggering the production of endorphins in the brain, which evokes feelings of

mind power.

(i) Memory Enhancement
(ii) Mind and self empowerment
(iii) Hormonal Balance
(iv) Joyful life

How to Do Blissful Neurobics

Mudra: GYAN MUDRA

Colour: VIOLET

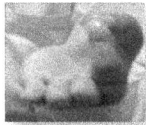

Procedure:

Step 1: Sit down comfortably either cross-legged or in the chair. Ensure your back is straight and hand gesture is in 'Dhyan Mudra'.

Step 2: Fold your tongue and touch the pallet and shut down your mouth.

Step 3: Visualise that you are inhaling violet coloured gas slowly and deeply. Now feel violet coloured showers entering through the Crown Chakra and spreading into whole body to give perfect relaxation to all cells and tissues of the body.

Step 4: Now exhale with a "Humming Sound" and feel that all black toxin gases are released. Also feel inner bliss with the humming sound.

Step 5: Now repeat the above steps for minimum 5 to 10 minutes. Practice slowly so that a stage must be reached when one act of respiration takes one minute.

DETAILS OF CROWN CHAKRA

Planet: Uranus, the universe

Power: Enlightenment

Related Body parts: The brain and the endocrinal glands

Relationship Style: Oneness & Unity

Emotional imbalances lead to – Apathy, Depression, Bigoted, Argumentative, Closed, Inability to learn, Unsocial, Careless, Lazy, Tired, Weakness, Low energy, Insomnia, Loss of memory

Alpha music, Creative work.

Daily Exercise: Head massage & Humming

Chakra closed by:

(i) Laziness

(ii) Ego

(iii) Discontentment

(iv) Drug addiction, Alcoholic drinks

(v) Excess medication

ENLIGHTENING NEUROBICS (ACTIVATING THIRD EYE [AJNA] CHAKRA ALSO CALLED KNOWLEDGE CHAKRA)

This Neurobic involves chanting vowels to create pure vibrations inside the brain to ignite and enlighten the mind with truth and knowledge. Most of the mantras in all religions are created

the last vowel). Humming after chanting "O" creates vibrations in the Agya Chakra.

Cures brain disorders, migraine, nerves and eye problems; stabilises the mind and the body in the beginning and ultimately strengthens the spirit. The purpose of chanting is to make our mind still and peaceful. Chanting provides emotional excitement and raises psychic energy to an intense level. It works as an instant energy booster.

1. Cures Brain Disorder
2. Increases Psychic Power
3. Cure eye disorder
4. Relief from Migraine
5. Relieves Nerves & Eye Disorder
6. Improves Eye Vision
7. Increases Memory & Mind Power
8. Enhances capacity to Discriminate from Real & Unreal to Balance Life

How to do Enlightening Neurobics

Mudra: PRAN MUDRA

Colour: INDIGO (Navy Blue)

Procedure:

Step 1: Sit down comfortably either crosslegged or in a chair. Ensure your back is straight and hand gesture is in "Pran Mudra'.

Step 2: Visualise that you are inhaling indigo colour (Navy blue) gases slowly and deeply.

Step 3: Now put your lips in "O" shape.

Step 4: Breathe out slowly and completely with "Oooo----" sound. While exhaling, feel that all black toxin gases are released.

Step 5: Repeat the above steps minimum for 5 to 10 minutes. OM or AUM is the most widely chanted phrase across religions and cultures. Some popular chants with Om resonating are Tibetan mantra – NamO Arihantanam NamO NamO and Sikh mantra Ek Omkar Satnam or Allah-O--- Akabar in Islam. This is the basic trinity of sounds and the whole music of life grows out of this.

Emotional imbalances lead to – Passive aggression, Fear, Flighty, Preoccupied, Nightmares.

Best Therapy: Rajyoga Meditation, Indigo Cosmic colour visualisation, Enlightening Neurobics,

Concentration on 3D images

Daily Exercise: Rub hands together vigorously, then place palms over your eyes and feel indigo showers from almighty God.

Related endocrinal – Pituitary gland

Chakra closed by

(i) Conditioning

(ii) Labeling

(iii) Judgments, like (I am this, you are that, life is this, I can't do this, it is not possible for me to do…..).

NEUROBIC SPA

Neurobic spa is a unique exercise of meditation in which we do meditation for clearing our whole   and for complete relaxation of mind.

In neurobic spa, we inhale seven colours related to virtues and clear all   of the body. The seven colours and the related virtues are given below:

Colours	Virtues
Violet	Bliss
Indigo	Knowledge and truth
Sky blue	Peace
Green	Love
Yellow	Joy
Orange	Purity
Red	Power

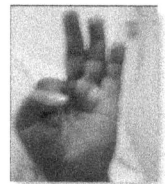

Steps or procedure to do this exercise:

1. Sit in a comfortable and relaxed position

3. And visualise the commentary mentioned below

Commentary for visualisation during Neurobic Spa (for 10 minutes only)

You are now about to embark upon the unique, wonderful and magical journey from darkness to light.

position and completely relax your body. Let your mind withdraw/avoid all your thoughts gradually passing by. Make no attempt to control it or stop it, let it is pass slowly….. simply observe them…

Now experience this wonderful transition, take a long deep breath and while doing so visualise

And when you breathe out... visualise the toxic gases of stress being forced out leaving you relaxed... calm, peaceful. Now breathe in deeply and breath out, keep visualising sparkling blue

Now experience a shining bright star, a tiny point of light shining at the centre of your forehead. You are seated right at the middle of your forehead, slowly start withdrawing all the energy from toes to your knees, from knees to your hips, from your hips to your lower back, further to your shoulders, and then to your neck. Now all the energy is focused at the spot...at the centre of your forehead. Your outer physical body is just like an empty shell or hollow object. Be void of your feelings and emotions.

You are now seated right at the middle of your forehead. Waiting for the shower of blessings coming forth from one and only almighty... Supreme God...our father...You are seated under a shower of vibrant and colourful rays....experiencing or feeling of ultimate bliss under the umbrella of colours...

Visualise the top of your Crown Chakra.... Slowly unfolding its petal, all the petals of the lotus opened up to receive this wonderful shower of blessings

Now sparkling red rays is entering through your Crown Chakra and go all the way down to your Root Chakra. The colour red which symbolises power, strengthening your bones and muscles making you strong and powerful. All the diseases associated with bones and the muscles of your body . . . are being disappeared....you are now emerging as a powerful soul.....

lower organs, bringing purity within you... all ailments associated with the lower organs of your body jave disappeared. And internally you are feeling light and pure. You are now a pure soul.

Bright and vibrant yellow coloured rays that symbolise joy and happiness enter through

digestive system, with abundant of joy and happiness. Thus cleaning and clearing all your sorrow, associated with unhappiness. You are now a happy and joyful soul.

Bright, beautiful and vibrant green colour – the symbol of love – enter through your Crown

Not only for yourself . . . .but for entire humanity....see your heart is pumping the bright green rays of love through your ventricles . . . your veins and arteries . . . your aorta is carrying the love to your energy cells of your body and internally spreading it all around you . . . now you are free from all the feelings of hatred and you become a loving soul.

Bright and vibrant sky blue colour rays of peace go through your Crown Chakra, down to your

removing all the traces of stress you now experience yourself as a being of peace. You are a peaceful soul.

cells with abundant of knowledge and truth. Visualise that all your brain cells have become activated and you are now a truthful and knowledgeable soul.

comes pouring down through your Crown Chakra and spreads all around your body creates a protective shield around you and makes you a blissful soul. This shower of blessings have fallen upon to carry it forth and bring about a positive transformation in the world; thus bringing about the difference to entire humanity.

You are now powerful . . pure . . . happy . . .loving . . .peaceful . . . truthful and a blissful soul.

and divine virtues . . . open your eyes and you experience yourself to have arrived to a new world . . . .

Chapter 2

CHECK YOUR MENTAL IMAGES

Is the mental image of your hand clear and steady or blurry and unstable? Is the picture three

is an effective way to enhance our mental creativity and versatility. Cognitive psychologists usually speak of the ability to visualise in terms of two factors.

1. Vividness
2. Controllability

Vividness means how bright, clear and lively an image appears.

Controllability means how steadily and responsively an image behaves.

Both are interrelated attributes. When you add vividness, your images are more colourful, realistic and three-dimensional. When you achieve controllability, your images are steadier and more precise.

Let's take a closer look at each of these qualities in the following examples:

1.

2. The great psychologist Francis Galeton devised a questionnaire that probed the clarity of people's visualisation power. Besides discovering that a few people are true eidetic imagers, Galeton discovered that people's visualisation skills do not improve easily. Here

a. Is your image clear or indistinct?

b. Is the image brighter or dimmer than the original scene?

    than others?

d. Does the image appear in colour or in shades of gray?

e. If your images are in colour, are the hues accurate?

f. Can you form a single visual image of the entire dining room?

g. Can you retain a steady image of your dinner plate? If so, does it grow brighter?

h. Can you mentally see your dinner plate, your hands holding a knife and fork, and a person's face sitting across from you all at the same time?

i. Can you feel the taste of the food?

j. Can you picture what were people wearing?

How did you do with these exercises? You have found that there are places in your imagination that are rich and vibrant, and places that are less clear. Perhaps you could visualise the people's face but not the shape of the cups. Maybe you could recreate the smell of the food but not the taste. Regardless of how vividly mental pictures can appear; our imagery tends to be far less accurate than we visualise it to be.

The accuracy of a mental image depends greatly on how much we have analysed the original objects. If you have never really examined a coin closely, you probably won't be able to form an accurate image of it. If you rarely give your dashboard a second glance, you won't have more than an abstract sense of what it looks like.

Use Your Graphic Analysis Muscles

To add life to your imagery, you need to sidestep verbal thinking and use your graphic analysis muscles.

Suppose you have to visualise something, what will you do? Begin by asking yourself what you actually see. Spend a moment looking at its shape, its origin and its relation to any other things. It means when you want to form a clear image, recall the key elements gleaned from your analysis– the sense of proportion and the arrangement of component shapes. Allow the

of visualising, but if you give yourself time, the images will grow brighter and steadier.

images emerge all at once, spontaneously, in full living colour, giving you a taste of how brightly and clearly mental picture may appear to an eidetic imager. More than anything else, the practice of forming sharp, accurate mental image strengthen your intellect's muscle and empower the third eye.

Various Neurobic exercises to tune mind and brain

1. **Visualisation of the real things:** Visualise each of the following items. If the images don't appear as bright as you want, don't try to force them into being. Instead focus on the idea of seeing an image, know that whatever you are trying to visualise has the shape, a texture, a colour, and a size. Take your own time to allow the image to become steady and sharp.

   Visualise the following:

   > A familiar face
   >
   > A sunset ocean
   >
   > A childhood friend
   >
   > Your bedroom
   >
   > A drop of dew
   >
   > A snow capped peak
   >
   > An ocean & its waves

2. **Visualisation of unrealistic things:**

   > A demigod with six arms
   >
   > A talking giraffe
   >
   > A chocolate river
   >
   > A thirty feet ant
   >
   > Visualise things begining with the letter A …..
   >
   > Visualise things that are larger than a bus
   >
   > Visualise things that are found under the ground
   >
   > Visualise things that make you happy

3. **Creating after images:** If you close your eyes after looking at an object, you will see an after image that lingers for a few moments. Try to incorporate this after image into your visualisation. For example: look at a pen. After seeing, close your eyes and see the after image. When the image fades, open your eyes, look at the pen and again start seeing its after image. Repeat this and after sometime you would be able to make the after image clearer and brighter.

4. **Using peripheral mental vision:** Visualise a pen in front of you. Then visualise it slowly making a circle around you. Gradually it is starting from left, coming back, coming to

right side of you, and starting from left, coming back, coming to right side of you, and again come in front. As the pen travels, visualise that you are using your peripheral vision to see it.

5. **Picturising people:** Visualise all the people you have spoken with today. What did they look like? What is the colour of eyes and hair, colour of clothes, heights and ages? Can you visualise their mannerisms and habits?

6. **Visualising Mathematical entities:** Visualise each of the following three dimensional shapes. Don't try just to form the image, also see the inner structure and relationships

   all sides: Spheres, Cube, Prism, Tetrahedron, Pyramid, Octahedron, etc.

7. **Visualising Feelings, nothing more than feelings:** Visualise a positive emotion.

   Try visualising a wish, without wishing for anything in particular. Visualise the emotions

   cotton, etc., and building materials like concrete, wood, tiles, etc., plants like oak tree rose petals, objects in a car like steering wheel, tape, deck, etc.

8. **Remaining present with intellect:** Form an image of presence of your mother, without actually seeing your mother; similarly summon a mental image of being in the presence of a mountain, without visualising the look of the mountain.

9. **Magnifying the body:** Try to see anything in a larger view. Visualise an ant like an elephant,

10. **Visualising Colours:**

    the colour, how bright can you make it? Try imagining colour blends, red to blue with intermediate shades in between. Thus you can increase your perfect imagination.

MENTAL COORDINATION

Goal setting exercise

Famous novelist Kurt Vonnegut has said, 'We are what we imagine ourselves to be.'

Here are some techniques to apply in neurobics to set your goal to avoid distractions.

1. **Goal visualisation:** Form a mental picture of yourself doing or having something that you want to have or want to do. In this exercise three things are important:
   a) Include details by engaging all your senses
   b) Visualise yourself enjoying the scenario you wish for yourself

   Encourage yourself to focus on objectives; help to stir up your motivation. Start with small easy to reach goals, and work up to larger ones.

2. **Visualising personal performance:** If you are going to give a presentation in a sales meeting, in a speech or in an interview, picture a range of possible scenarios, begin with

an ideal outcome.

Visualise you are performing in top shape with things happening exactly as you want them to be. Then visualise the worst possible outcome with you stumbling over yourself. In the process of rehearsing these scenarios you prepare yourself for mishaps and problems.

Once you have worked through the possibilities, focus on the ideal images. Allow yourself to perform marvellously.

3. **Relaxation:** Take some time to recall pleasant memories. Relax your body and let your

close friends, early childhood, your old room, walking to school in the sun, snow or rain, etc.

4. **Visualise inner messages:** Visualise a blackboard in the upper left hand corner, watch the letters of your name appearing slowly, one at time. Then in the upper right hand corner of the blackboard watch the letter of word 'relax' appearing one at a time. Pause for a moment and look at the words. Then go one line down, watch the word appear again. Create an inner message appearing on the board in very bold letters, which stirs your mind and motivates you.

5. **Calming the emotions:** Swami Dayananda Saraswati, a Sanskrit teacher, has an interesting application for mental imagery. To help let go of the inner agitation associated with a troubling situation, focus on the positive. For example, if you are angry with your boss, visualise your boss doing something you like. Recall a time when he/she did something you approved of. Keep looking for the positive. Be willing to accept your boss as he/she is. Though you may not approve of all of his/her actions, don't feel compelled to change or to mentally mar him/her. Apply this technique to domestic quarrels also. This

DECISION MAKING

To make wise decision, it is helpful to have a method for evaluating options that includes both rational and emotional factors. Feelings, beliefs, values and attitudes as well as facts should play key roles in our decisions. Following steps will lead to an effective decision making:

(A) State your purpose: To make the best decision we need to know clearly what we want. We need to give ourselves a target. Figuring out just exactly what needs to be determined should

essence of the situation and restrict the range of solution.

Formulating a broad statement of purpose also helps us to distinguish between means and end.

They represent the activities and techniques that help us reach ends. Something can become a means or an end depending on the context of our purpose.   A job can be a means

(B) Establish Criteria: For clarifying our statement of purpose, we should determine the

I. What do I want to achieve?

II. What do I want to preserve?

III. What do I want to avoid?

Your response to these questions become a yardstick that will measure how well possible alternatives stack up against each other and ultimately lead you to your best course of action.

For example: If you have a purpose to determine the best way to buy a car, you might arrive at the following list of criteria:

a) **Achieve:** A dependable car, with a good repair record and a long warranty. Get a sporty car or one that makes heads turn or get a comfortable car which provides lots of space for passengers or get a responsive car, which has plenty of power and good handling.

b) **Preserve:**
target should be to get a car that has good gas mileage, low insurance premium and a good resale value.

c) **Avoid:** Avoid costly repairs. Parts should be readily available and reasonably priced and the car should perform reliably.

set an upper price tag of Rs 5 lakhs. You could specify that the car must be bright red and so on.

Examine your criteria to determine whether they contradict each other. Do you want a luxury car for fewer than 4 lakhs? Do you want a car with tremendous performance but very high gas mileage?

Once you have settled on an assortment of criteria, set priorities. To each criterion, assign a number from one to ten, with ten representing the most important criterion and one representing the least important criterion.   If performance is most important to you, it rates ten. If the cost of the car is less important then it might get a rating of eight. If repair costs seem

In the rating phase, you determine what is important and what is not so important. Select at

and give it a rating of ten. Rank the other criteria, as desirable objectives, which would be nice to achieve, but are not critical.

cost of the car becomes more important than the air conditioning. At the end of process you

This is just an example of buying a car. You can follow the same steps for establishing criteria to set your desired goals or objectives.

(C) Search for alternatives: After you have determined your criteria – what you want to achieve, preserve and avoid, You need to think about possible courses of action. The key to
To search for

year warranty, and comes in bright red. With this question in mind you can look in newspapers, magazines, and showrooms and build a list of cars that will satisfy at least some of these criteria. Too many times we choose alternatives before we set our criteria. Let your criteria generate your alternatives.

(D) Evaluating and testing alternatives: Having listed your alternatives, the next step in the decision-making process is to compare how each alternative stacks up against the other. In some

all your criteria. But in other cases each alternative holds advantages and disadvantages. In situations like these, you need to rank your alternatives. Compare each alternative to each criterion. Unless new information and new alternatives appear, carry through the decision that you have made. Avoid the tendency to switch just before the moment of action.

(E) Choose and feel: There is a popular story about Albert Einstein. When confronted with a decision that had two possible alternatives (a yes or no decision or this or that decision),

When the coin landed, he would look at the face of the coin and immediately ask himself how

with the other alternative.

MIND CONTROL TECHNIQUES

Simple neurobics to turn the unguided mind into a guided mind

All problems of a human being are due to his own unguided mind. Problem of stress,

diseases in human body which further results in unbridled mind.

are driving a car, then there is no doubt that you are a driver. If you cannot differentiate yourself from the car, you cannot drive the car. Similarly, if a rider cannot differentiate himself from the

step to have guided mind is to be aware of the true self – the Being and not the human (Body) which has to be driven. Here the body can be compared to the car and the Being – the soul can be compared to the driver.

The following mental exercises (Simple neurobics) are needed to develop a great will to guide your unguided mind and develop the necessary awareness:

1. **Awareness of what steers the mind:** Suppose you are driving a car, the driver is in the front wheel which are guided by the STEERING and the DRIVE SHAFT. The drive shaft further depends on steering. You get control over these with the two front wheels: the rest of the car is actually not in control. Yet you are able to direct the car to go where you want to go. By just taking the STEERING wheel in your hands, not even with both the hands, just one hand – still the car goes where you want it to go.

The same is true with self. If the Real self – the being – just takes charge of its own steering wheel and steers it properly, everything else goes with it. If you try to take charge of all the bits and pieces of this human car into your control, if you start thinking in terms of what could be happening with all the different parts of the human car, you will go crazy. So, you do not have to take the whole mind into your control that is not necessary. With spiritual process you do not have to grasp everything. If you try to take every cell in your body, every atom in one direction, you will go crazy; you will not take anything anywhere. Same way when you approach the subjective dimensions of life intellectually, this is what happens; you are trying to take charge of everything. This is not necessary. You just take the steering wheel in your hands, you keep it steady and it will go where you want. It will not go anywhere else.

So how much your mind is in your control is not relevant. The essential part is – RIGHT CONSCIOUNSNES. That is enough. Rest of it follows anyway, it can't go anywhere, else.

2. **Awareness of simple tools for driving the human car (Steering the mind):** To learn driving a car you need not be a mechanic or undergo a full course to know each and every part of a car. You can learn driving by simple awareness of the tools of driving and practicing driving for a few days.

   Same way to steer the mind you need not to be a spiritualist or ascetic or a religious leader or offer prayers daily to God. But you just need simple awareness of truth and living a practical life with right consciousness.

3. **Knowledge of how to steer the mind or guide the unguided mind**

   Techniques of driving a human car:

   about the basic rules of driving and then you are asked to start the practice. In the same way there are the following rules of driving the human car by the Being – Driver.

   Rule I: Sit on the driver seat and tighten the belt.

   That means visualise yourself as a Being – the soul (see as a point of light or a shining star) and position yourself between the eyes in the forehead. After positioning on the seat, tighten the belt of strong determination for quick and effective learning.

   Rule II:

   That means create a positive and powerful thought. Only positive thought is not going to help. It has to be powerful.

   Suppose you smell a dead rat in your room and spray scents in your room to cover the stinking smell of dead rat. This will be a shorttime effect. The stinking smell will start coming when the effect of scents vanishes. You have to have the power to locate the rat and throw it outside and then spray the scents. Same way positive thoughts are like scents which does not have lasting effects. You have to have positive and powerful thoughts.

   Either this thought should come from your sub-conscious or unconscious mind or should be put in your mind (That is right consciousness) by your teacher who is teaching you the driving. Some 'Guru" gives some mantra to their disciple for "japa" (chanting) but that is not the right consciousness because later on this mantra merely becomes mechanical and mind keeps wandering but mouth keeps repeating the mantra. That is of no use. A few examples of right consciousness are:

1. I am the powerful soul and I can turn the tide in my favour.
2. I am the victorious soul and defeats cannot stop my journey.
3. I am the master of my mind and intellect. I will use them in the right way only.
4. I am the real leader and I will lead my fellow beings on right path to a right destination.
5. I am the most effective manager. Not only I can manage myself in any challenging situations but can deliver the best also.
6. I am an immortal soul. I cannot die. Death of body does not mean an end but a restart of another journey.
7. I am the most obedient son of my supreme father (God); I cannot violate any law of nature.
8. I am the merciful soul and I have empathy and sympathy for all ignorant souls.
9. I am the richest soul with imperishable treasures of virtues and will power and nothing can attract me and deviate me from my right path.
10. I am the right judge and my judgment is based on values and principles. I am proud of my right decision and I will execute my decision at any cost.

There are many more positive and powerful thoughts which can steer the mind or right consciousness and which have steered many minds to a victory.

Rule III: Start the engine in neutral gear; that means see your physical body in quiet comfortable and neutral gear. That means you are mentally present to go ahead for driving process.

Rule IV:
waste and negative thoughts coming from impressions of subconscious mind. Then

consciousness (positive & powerful thoughts).

Rule V: Slowly start accelerating and releasing pressures slowly from clutch and move

accelerates the powerful thoughts and release slowly waste and negative emotional impressions from conscious mind.

Rule VI: Now drive the car a short distance at slow speed. That means steer the mind on the road of positive personality with a fully conscious state of powerful attitude.

Rule VII: Again press clutch and change to second gear. That means again suppress the disturbing waste and negative impression which are diluting the powerful thoughts and then recollect the positive and powerful impressions from subconscious mind (Trigger any successful moment of past from memory) which can further empower the right consciousness to move further and faster on the road map of positive personality.

Rule VIII: Again press the clutch and change to top (Third) gear. It means nullifying the

Various Mind Management Techniques

waste and negative impressions from consciousness and motivating self with powerful impressions of your true nature (That is truth, peace, love, happiness, bliss, purity & power) of the being – the soul. And then accelerate with pure and powerful emotions with high speed and drive correctly on the path of positive personality.

Rule IX: This is a golden rule. Keep checking the speed of the vehicle with powerful brake system to avoid over speeding and accidents.

It means driving on the path of positive personality and not getting obstructed with

scenes of glory and pleasures. Here you need to apply the brakes of will power of intellect and recreate the right consciousness with creative skills of intellect, to keep moving forever on right path of positive personality, to the destination of perfect personality.

Rule X: Keep checking the fuel and oil availability and serviceable condition of the

by physical exercise to keep the body in serviceable condition.

Here balanced diet does not mean taking non-vegetarian foods. Non-veg diet never makes a personality a positive one. Our mind gets affected by food. "As the food so is the mind", therefore, it is advisable to take vegetarian diet. Even human body structure also does not permit a non-veg diet. A study of human anatomy and physiology also reveals that a human is a vegetarian animal.

DEVELOPING WILL POWER

What is will power?

There will be various factors in the stories of men's success and failures of life but in every single case there will be one common factor involved. That is the factor of will power. The degree of a person's success in life is commensurate with the degree of will power he has attained.

It is the positive and creative function of the objective mind, which impels, propels and enables

known to be wrong, under all circumstances favourable or unfavourable.

Why develop will power?

Self-empowerment is almost impossible without the voluntary or involuntary exercise of the will power. Development of will power is necessary for the following reasons:

1. **Turning failure into success:** Given the will power, man makes everything out of nothing, as it were. In the absence of will power all his talents and qualities and endowments come to nothing. Consider these three cases of modern history:

   If we study the lives of those persons who were once in very bad shape and afterwards were found to have risen from the shambles, we shall discover in every single case, it was their will power that brought about their transformation, rise and success.

2. **Turning a tragedy into a strategy:** Sometimes in our lives, great tragedies happen. They shake us to our roots. After that tragedy we are never the same persons again. These tragedies are such that we are forced to take agonising notice of them. We become objects of real pity. This is about the big tragedies of our personal lives. If we know how to take these tragedies creatively, we are largely transformed. Without a strategy we are crushed in a tragedy.

3. **To use the power of words:** We know it is good to use polite, decent and restrained language in our daily dealings at home, on the street, in business, in politics, in society. Despite this awareness, we use wrong language, from which arise many small and big dissensions at home, in society, in national and international affairs. Very often we do not remember the power of words, their capacity to break or make, wound or heal. More often, our will just fails to carry into practice what we know about the power of words. Through use of wrong language we are apt to make such wounds in other's hearts as it will not be easily healed; or we may anger people to such an extent that dire consequences may follow, and we ourselves shall have to reap them, however bitter they may be.

4. **To desist from sinful acts:**
of ourselves, we commit sinful acts. And having committed them we have to take their painful consequences. We can give away our entire property but there is no way of giving away the fruits of our   . We shall have to enjoy or suffer them ourselves. We know it is good to get up early in the morning and practice spiritual disciplines. But when in the morning the alarm clock dutifully rings, we feel annoyed and silence it as though it had committed some crime, and then pull the blanket over to nose the sleep half an hour more, only to hurry and worry all day long. In the evening when we return home we are a mass

5. **To get rid of laziness and bad habits:** We may observe, even in little thing how little

On the contrary we continue to do harmful things. We know it is not good to neglect our studies but somehow we cannot turn our ears or eyes from the radio or TV specially when a cricket match, a circus show, a fashion show or a movie is going on. If our mind timidly protests we just give it a trashing: how can I miss such an exciting thing for the boring bla-bla bla of my classes? And the consequences of it are too obvious in the evergrowing restlessness and dissatisfaction among the youngsters.

Don't people very well know that it is not good to drink alcohol? Still they gulp one or

to break the promise again; ultimately they fail to keep their promises. Therefore only a powerful will can change these bad habits.

6. **To resist our temptation:** We know that being over-weight is a health hazard and we should avoid eating too many sweets and other highly fattening things. But when these things come around, we smile on our own mental decision and oppositions of well wishers. It is well-known that some of us can resist everything except temptations. There is a great fascination in the prohibited, great attraction in the destructive, great pull in the

bizarre and wicked things in this world. They pull us by the ear and make slaves of us. We do things in a hurry. They pull us by the ear and make slaves of us. We do things in a hurry and then repent at leisure and weep in the darkness of our own making.

Steps for developing will power

With self-realisation we empower ourselves to direct our objective minds to accept only positive and powerful thoughts to program our memories (subjective minds) to replace negative and

will power starts with self-realisation only. Following steps are necessary to develop a great will-power:

1. **Introspection:** Introspection means inspecting the inner self. That is about our strengths and weaknesses. One's personal strengths are those aspects of life which are really good and working well and weakness are those aspects of life which are not so good and are causing sorrow or discomfort to us.

   Let me be clearer on strength. Recollect the memories of past happenings events and

   in order to be successful and on which he can depend on in the future too. Introspection is the spiritual wisdom, which is the missing dimension in our present life. Introspection is also called spiritual insights to know and understand about the inner organisation. Inner organisation has two aspects:

   a) The innate self or the real self

   b) The acquired self or the physical self. That is whatever we have acquired after coming to this world. That is ego, the role, image, possessions, skills, body relationship, position, achievements, beliefs, etc.

   * (About the real self, you must read and understand one of the most important chapters of this book- "self concept")

2. **Observation of our own thoughts pattern:** The second step for development of will power is to start observing the thought patterns specially related to waste and negative

   reduced automatically because we become conscious of the self as soul and treat our mind as one of our obedient faculties. Thoughts keep coming till we are involved with mind and intellect to feel emotions and react according to the thoughts. Once we start feeling ourselves as a spirit (soul) and as a master of our mind and intellect, we become the authority and start becoming assertive and proactive rather than reactive and aggressive according to our thoughts pattern. Here one can visualise that the famous personality and one's role model (you should select your role model) standing in front of self and telling following words (feel than you can listen to these words):

   "Stand up, be bold, be strong. Know that you are the creator of your own destiny. All the strength and succour you want is within yourself!"

   Repeatedly visualise this and hear each word and feel the emotion of each word and also

truth. No one is destined to be weak all his life except him who chooses to be so. A determined effort is possible at one's chosen time for a departure to the better, nobler, higher state of existence. It is never too early or too late to be good, pure, true and strong.

3. **Connecting self to intellect to create a new belief system in our memory bank:** After becoming a spectator and realising one's own true identity, now connect self to intellect

Thus by this powerful connection create a new faith or new belief system in the memory. Assert yourself, be brave, take courage in both hands and follow the truth to its logical conclusion. Go with truth wherever it takes us: that should be our motto because truth only helps us to develop clear focus in our life. Opposition to this way of thinking and living will, most certainly come. We must predetermine a proper attitude to such opposition and

If possible, again visualise your role model standing in front of you and asking you, "Have you got the will to surmount the mountain's high obstruction? If the whole world stands against you with a sword in hand, would you still dare to do what you think is right? If your wives and children are against you, if all your money goes, your name dies, your wealth vanishes, would you still stick to it? Would you still pursue it and go steadily towards the goal?" It is with this temper, we shall have to face opposition for the development of a great will power. The love for truth and temper for facing the opposition will spontaneously develop within, with the above visualisation repeatedly.

4. **Develop a clear focus:** A clear focus is required to guide our life activities on the basis of a clear sense of purpose, values and vision. The purpose of our life has to be understood from various perspectives. Life can be centred on work, money, power, family or society and there are many ways to make those short-term gains. The main purpose of our life is to lead a meaningful life. Purpose becomes the basis of our will for excellence. It gives

the focus and then enables us to apply spiritual wisdom of how to channelise the innate powers and capabilities towards those things which are meaningful, instead of just wasting the energy.

5. **Set a routine:** On the basis of whatever you have thus learnt and determined you should yourself plan simple routines for your daily life. The routine should be planned keeping in view that you are seeking daily self-preservation and self-improvement at all levels, physical, mental, social, and spiritual. It should be so planned that our human relations, recreational need, ideals and aspirations, everything could be actualised through those routines. No matter what happens, we should follow that routine. In the preliminary stage

our decisions. Exceptional cases may arise when the routine will have to be set aside, for instance, when there is a serious accident in the house or any death or any celebrations, etc., but as soon as possible we should return to our routine. At a later stage when we have

according to the higher needs of our self development.

6. **Start your day with meditation or prayer:** According to psychologists, human memory is so powerful in the early morning hours, that it absorbs the input like a blotting paper. Some people have the capacity to absorb for half an hour for some it is 45 min, one hours, two hours, three hours depending from individual to individual when the memory reaches a saturated state, it does not absorb any further. So we have to be very selective especially in the morning hours when the memory is in a high state of absorbing. We have to be cautious of the quality of nourishment we are giving to our memory because accordingly our entire system will function. When one nourishes one's mind with healthy positive inputs during early morning in meditation to empower oneself, spiritual dimensions is the only source of quality information of knowledge which generates will power to take the focus of control in one's own hand. Meditation is thus a technique of inculcating or imbibing or nourishing one's intellect with positive visualisation of values application with self, thus our complete inner mechanism starts changing.

Following Rajyoga (mind-body-soul) exercises daily (early in the morning) is advised for developing a great will power:

"I am a powerful soul… I feel the rays of cosmic power in red colour falling on me… I concentrate on the rays… I feel the rays of divine power entering into the cells and tissues of bones and muscle… I see a bright light… He is almighty and powerful… I see red rays of power falling on my whole body…I feel powerful, the rays are entering into the body… all cells and tissues are charged … I feel complete powerful…My body has become red like 'Mahabir-Hanuman'…I am now empowered by divine energy to do any impossible act possible…My problems are now opportunities for me to prove myself powerful in this world…God is on my side and victory is mine…Success is my birth right and none can snatch this from me…I am radiating powerful rays all around through my eyes… Om Shanti, Om Shanti, Om Shanti."

Comprehensive Memory Development Course

Chapter 3

S leep is the most important factor for healthy living. Optimum hours of sleep one should

SCIENTIFIC FACTS ABOUT SLEEP

1. We sleep in cycles of 90 to 120 minutes each and our EEG (Electro Encephalo Graph),

    50% of each sleep cycle in light/ very light sleep, next 30% in deep/ very deep sleep and rest 20% of the cycle in REM (Rapid Eye Movements) sleep (known as dream sleep).

2. We need to have a total of 45 to 50 minutes of delta waves to feel totally fresh after sleep.

    cycle carries 5 to 10 minutes of delta waves only. After third cycle, delta waves are not produced at all.

3. Sleeping after third cycle is either due to habit or for psychological satisfaction. But it is a waste of time because it never gives you relaxation, instead it drains out gained energy during three cycles and people feel tired even after sleeping more.

4. Sleep after third cycle is called half sleep or dream sleep, which produces more theta waves, which is a low amplitude wave with low frequency. One needs to sleep only for

    next 12 hours. After 12 hours only, you will need to sleep one cycle, which again can freshen up for next 4 hours.

5. During deep sleep we sleep completely in delta waves, where as in theta wave sleep (Dream sleep) our mind still works with imaginations but intellect does not function with its controlling power. Therefore, sleep means complete sleep with minimum 45 minutes of delta waves.

For example: Suppose you are climbing a mountain while awake, you stop after reaching on top. But during sleep you climb non-stop and feel you are falling from the top you wake up thereafter and you feel the same reaction on your face as it happened in reality.

BRAIN WAVES CHART

Brain waves are measured by an instrument named EEG. It measures electrical activities of the brain cells by placing electrodes on the scalp.

S. No.	Brain waves	Frequency	State of mind
1.	Beta	More than 14 Hz (cycles actively per sec)	Mind is alert and awake, busy in worldly activities.
2.	Alpha	8 – 13 Hz	Mind awake but relaxed, eye closed.
3.	Theta	4 – 8 Hz	Drowsiness, Dream state.
4.	Delta	0.5 – 4 Hz	Deep sleep.

HOW TO MANAGE SLEEP

Do the following to manage your sleep in the best possible way:

1. **Short nap during the day time for 15 to 30 minutes:** A short nap of 15 to 30 minutes during daytime produces low theta waves and sometimes delta waves for 5 minutes, which refreshes us for next 4 to 6 hours.

2. **Relaxation technique:** Relaxation techniques produces alpha waves which further reduces the rate of draining gained energy during delta wave sleep and keeps us cool and energetic.

3. **Rajyoga Meditation:** The theta and delta state of mind is achieved by Rajyoga meditation in which mind remains fully awake but cut off from external world or sense organ perceptions

Half an hour of meditation can give the relaxation equal to one cycle of sleep and refreshes us for the next six hours. 15 to 20 minutes of meditation can refresh for next three to four hours. It reduces the duration of our sleep cycles to 90 minutes. Meditation also activates our pituitary gland (Master gland) to release 17 hormones harmoniously in our bodies.

BEST POSSIBLE SLEEPING PATTERNS

Following sleeping patterns are advised to manage your sleep as per your job requirement:

1. **10 pm to 4 am:** If you remain very busy, it is advised to go to bed at 10 am and get up early in the morning. You can use this golden time to do the neurobic exercises of body-mind-soul and recharge yourself with positive energy for whole day activities.

2. **11 pm to 5 am :** If you are able to have a short nap of 20-30 minutes, you can take one hour extra in your hand and go to bed at 11 pm. You can do the neurobic exercises after getting up to rejuvenate with positive energy.

3. **Two cycles of sleep during night and one cycle during day:** If you get time during the day for full one cycle of sleep, it is advised to sleep only two cycles of sleep during night time. Extra sleeping will reduce the energy and make life dull.

4. **One cycle of sleep during night and two cycles during day:** If you are a night worker, it is advised to have at least one cycle of sleep during night time and two cycles of sleep during day time. Full three cycles of sleep is not advisable during day time due to presence of negative energy all around.

between these periods.

NEUROBICS FOR MANAGING SLEEP

Do the following body-mind-soul exercise to get instant relaxation and manage your sleep by reducing duration of one sleep cycle to 90 minutes:

"See yourself as a point of light as shining star between forehead… Feel the light of the soul is spreading into whole face… See the light is further expanding into your whole body through neck, chest, stomach, arms, lower abdomen and both legs… See the inner body is bright inside and covered by skin from outside... Feel the focus of light into whole body and try to see all your organs inside... Now feel that there is a violet coloured shower from overhead source of divine light, which is entering into your whole body through Crown Chakra, face, neck, chest, stomach, arms, lower abdomen and both legs. Feel that you are completely relaxed… All cells and tissues are charged with divine powers… And you have become fully relaxed, blessed by God and ready to take on the day with love, courage and smile. Open your eyes and radiate blissful rays of lights through your eyes all around.

PART : IV

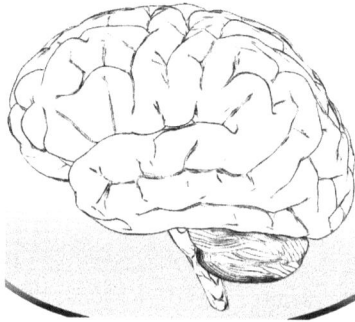

BRAIN MASSAGING TECHNIQUES

Chapter 1

1. **Revision:** Revision is very necessary for retention of something one has memorised. Without revision, one cannot retain the required things for a long time. Suppose you have memorised something. Now the question arises when should one revise for retaining it in the memory?

   to retain any fresh information up to 80-100% only for 24 hours. After that it goes down and gets linked with already existing information that one has. The forgetting cycle speeds up by

   Once the fresh information is revised after 24hrs, the brain has the capacity to hold it for approximately next seven days. After that one must revise the topics for a second time so that it is permanently memorised for a long time. Follow this procedure for a month. After a month you can revise it fortnightly and then monthly.

   If you follow these time periods, your revision time will be only 10% of your total time. You will require only twelve minutes revising the entire topic because you do not need any note books to revise it. Your memory bank is the moving note book for you. Revision

2. **Use both sides of your brain:** Medical science says that the left side of the brain deals with logic, language, numbers and sequence, while the right side is connected with visualisation of images, colour and awareness. However, both hemispheres of the brain can undertake all kinds of activities. You should never say that you do not have the capacity to imagine or that you are weak in a certain subject. In fact, the logical answer is that you have not developed an interest in that particular subject. All you have to do is improve your memory in order to use both sides of the brain. As you get older you lose your imaginative skills. In other words, you use less of your right brain hemisphere. Take the case of children studying in lower classes. They cram classroom walls with coloured drawings. They have boxes full of coloured pencils, paints, etc. When they reach higher classes, they are on the move, from one room to another and visual stimulation is absent. Most of them stop learning in the new environment.

   The lesson to be learnt here is that if we want a powerful memory, we have to retain material in the brain so effectively that we can recall it after an hour or even after a year.

Brain Sharpening Techniques

HOW TO USE BOTH PARTS OF BRAIN

The human brain is a paired organ; it is composed of two halves, called cerebral hemisphere. The theory of the structure and functions of the brain suggests that the two sides of the brain are related to two different modes of thinking. Just stop to wonder for a moment how a two-year old baby can master the task of speaking so effortlessly while most adult efforts at learning a foreign language tend to end up as more effort and less learning. Most children are born with right hemisphere dominant, when an infant learns a language; he/she does so with all his/her senses of smell, sounds, colours, feelings, etc. As we grow older, the left hemisphere modes of thinking which rely heavily on partial processes (without visualisations) of the intellect (logic, sequence, and organisation) become dominant.

In the Zen tradition, the left mind is associated with the process of thinking and the right mind is associated with knowing. Most individuals tend to have a distinct preference for one or the other side of the brain. From very early in life, school and society too conspire to identify individual as one or the other (Arts or the Science) and label them as "Creative or logical".

USING THE OTHER HAND

It has been established that the right brain, which is connected with a person's intuitive, creative and holistic faculties, is linked to left hand movements, while the left brain whose functions are logical, analytical and rational is linked to right hand movements. Thanks to the over-emphasis on the written word and paperwork, all of which are left brain activities done with the right hand. The chances are that schooling has left you with a lopsided brain development. Such acts like brushing our teeth or combing our hair with the non-dominant hand (in the most cases the left) if incorporated into our routine can help stimulate the creative brain.

DO FAMILIAR TASKS DIFFERENTLY

Try showering or starting the car with your eyes shut or read a page or two upside down, or simply shut the eyes for a few minutes and explore the room with the other senses – touch, smell, background noises, etc., to tune into the right brain. These simple acts force you out of the most frequently utilised areas of your mind and into areas less utilised.

PICTURE THE PROBLEM

Stuck on the problem and with nowhere to go? Try depicting it pictorially – yes, drawing it out, using colours to depict its intensity or aspects, arrows to depict its direction, anything goes. Drawing or attempting to visually depict a problem or its solution can trigger off the brain into alternate neurological pathways to come up with better and more holistic ideas.

MENTAL GAME

Some of the simple games we played as children can help tone up the brain and reinforce the functions of sequential thinking, logic and the remembering of names and dates, crossword puzzle, etc., offer an excellent mental workout as does a good round of scrabble.

MOVING BODY

Our bodies are very much a part of all our learning and learning is not an isolated brain function. Every nerve cell is a network contributing to our intelligence and our learning capability. Complex movement stimulates complex thinking. Across the body arm movements such as those used in swimming or doing the march-past stimulate brain synchronisation and help develop better communication across the hemisphere. Rhythmic movements such as dancing, skating, walking or martial arts also serve to stimulate the brain into activating more complex pathway.

Improve functioning of the right brain hemisphere by following mental/physical exercises

1. Visualise your organisation/home/yourself/spouse 10 years from now.

3. Design a logo for your job and family.
4. Make decisions based on intuition/gut feeling.
5. Conceptualise a new product.
6. Listen to music.
7. Take decisions as a team.
8. Convert words into pictures. Write a letter only through pictures (or with minimum words).
9. Learn to make a new dish.
10. Play with children the way they want to play.
11. Be with nature; enjoy watching the moon, trees, leaves, and breeze.
12. Become spiritual (not necessarily religious).
13. Thank people, be grateful.

Improving the left brain hemisphere by following mental/physical exercises

1. Learn a new computer programme.

3. Prepare a time log.

5. Prepare a "to do" list and tick off things as you do them.
6. Plan a project and execute it in stages.
7. Be on time for appointments.
8. Use logic, probabilities, and data in decision making.
9. Write down all aspects of a practical retirement life.
10. Play logic games.
11. Assemble a model kit by following the instructions.

13. Prepare a family tree.
14. Keep things neat and tidy in proper places.
15. Write down expiry dates of your driving license, insurance policy, etc.
16. Write down advantages and disadvantages of a product decision and quantify them.
17. Complete tasks on time.

Chapter 2

Dr. Paul Nogier, a neurologist, during his 20 long years of research from 1950 to about 1970 discovered that the ears correspond to the inverted fetus curled in the womb (emerging human body). The ear lobes corresponding to the left and the right brain. This fact was already known to the ancient Chinese acupuncturists and the great   in India.

The 'principle of ear acupuncture' was also discovered by the great Indian sages (rishis) while studying the life style in the Golden Age and the Silver Age of India and developed a technique to increase the intelligence level. Ear rings were worn as a common ornament by male as well as females.

However, the precise technique has been distorted and lost now. The human body is like complicated and subtle electronic equipment. The right ear lobe corresponding to the left brain and the left lobe corresponding to the right brain.

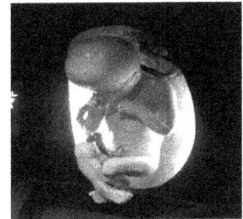

This Neurobic exercise transforms the lower energies to higher frequencies and brings them up to the upper energy centres. This transformation improves the memory

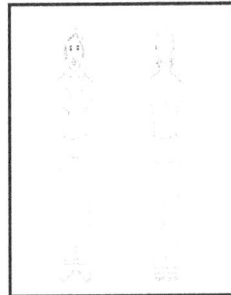

Brain Balancing by Dynamic Neurobics

STEPS FOR DYNAMIC NEUROBICS

Step 1: Activate Left Brain – gently squeese the right ear lobe with the left thumb placed outside

activating and energising the Left brain and the Pituitary gland.

Step 2: Activate Right brain – gently squeezing the left ear lobe with the right thumb placed

connection energising and activating the Right brain and the Pineal gland.

Step 3: Connect the energy channels – the front energy channel is broken in the mouth area since the body has to eat. To complete the energy wiring in the front and back energy channels, touch the pallet by the tip of the tongue. This causes the front and back energy channels to expand by 5 to 10 millimeters in diameter.

Step 4:

the divine source for divine blessings. Latent powers are gradually awakened within us also involving internal alchemy. Divine rays of Indigo colour energise the brain and the complete nervous system.

Step 5: Start squatting down while inhaling and standing up while exhaling. 70 (For the aged or physically handicapped) Semi squatting is advisable. They can do Dynamic Neurobics in semi squat position though it is not as powerful as full Squatting; therefore the number of times has to be increased – 50 to 70 times per session).

Step 6:

Duration: Repeat 14 times per session.

DIRECTIONAL PREFERENCE

East Direction: East direction is for children, teenagers and adults with a strong and basic energy.

East radiates predominantly 'Violet' pranic energy activating the upper energy centres. It brings up energies from the basic and sex energy centres to the upper energy centres.

North Direction: North Direction is for older people with weak and depleted sex and basic energy centres. There are less of lower energies to be transformed to higher energies to be utilised by the upper energy centres and the brain. North radiates predominantly 'Red' pranic energy strengthening the lower energy centres.

To improve intelligence: Repeat 21 times per session. For   , or advanced meditation: Repeat 7 times per session only.

Precautions:

pranic energy level of the brain is higher and the effect is more powerful.

2. Correct arm position: The right arm must be outside and the left arm must come under it. This applies to both male and female. This helps activate and energize the brain. It is seen clairvoyantly as the brain becomes more luminous.

    IMPORTANT: If the right arm is inside and the left arm outside, it causes a "Short circuit" depleting and dimming the brain. Put it in a box

3. Females should not perform this Neurobics 2 days before, 2 days after and during

    the dirty energy to the upper energy centres and the brain.

4. If a person's sex energy centre and basic energy centre are dirty, it is better for the practitioner to clean the centre by practicing light Neurobics and Raj Yoga before practicing the Dynamic Neurobics.

5. Do not smoke. Smoking makes the physical body and energy body dirty. It causes heart problems, hypertension and other problems.

6. Avoid alcohol as it is physically and psychologically detrimental to a person and at the same time harmful to one's family also. Addictive or hallucinogenic drugs must be avoided because they make the energy body dirty and damage the physical body.

7. Avoid eating non-vegetarian diets. As they are very dirty for the energy centres.

8. It is important to keep the body clean and not overdo this exercise to avoid or minimise possible physical health problems like – Insomnia, Overheating of the body, Weakening of the body, Pain & discomfort, Skin rashes, etc.

Afterword

This book has comprehensively explained the right concept

the function of head top computer, a term coined by Dr BK Chandra Shekhar. This book also explains how to memorise faster and effectively. Almost all methodology and technologies have been explained thoroughly. Digit codes with pictures up to 1000 have been given, which is very useful for all, and especially for CA, CS & LLB Students.

I strongly recommend this book for all students and

development.

I congratulate Dr Chandra Shekhar for bringing this book very nicely and comprehensively for

My best wishes to the author and readers....

Prof. Dr. S Viswanathan

MD, DGO, FRCS, FIMSA, FABMS, PGDY, PGD (VE & S), PGD (Memory Development & Psycho Neurobics), PGD (YOGA THERAPY), M Sc (YOGA), Ph. D, Professor & HOD (Obs & Gyn), Medical Superintendent & Director (Annamallai University)

– Dr. S Viswanathan
Email: viswayoga@gmail.com

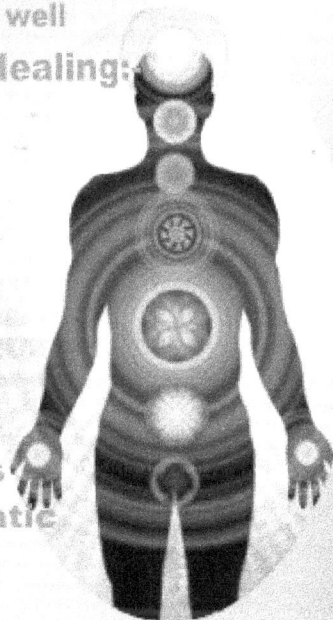

www.ingramcontent.com/pod-product-compliance
Lightning Source LLC
Chambersburg PA
CBHW082351270326
41935CB00013B/1579